D1601351

CIVIL OBEDIENCE

CIVIL OBEDIENCE

AN ORAL HISTORY

OF SCHOOL DESEGREGATION

IN FAYETTEVILLE, ARKANSAS

1954–1965

JULIANNE LEWIS ADAMS

THOMAS A. DeBLACK

WITH AN INTRODUCTION BY
WILLARD B. GATEWOOD

THE UNIVERSITY OF ARKANSAS PRESS · 1994

99   98   97   96   95   5   4   3   2   1

DESIGNED BY ELLEN BEELER

THE PAPER USED IN THIS PUBLICATION MEETS THE MINIMUM REQUIREMENTS OF THE
AMERICAN NATIONAL STANDARD FOR PERMANENCE OF PAPER FOR PRINTED LIBRARY
MATERIALS Z39.48-1984. ∞

LIBRARY OF CONGRESS CATALOGING-IN-PUBLICATION DATA

ADAMS, JULIANNE LEWIS, 1965–
    CIVIL OBEDIENCE: AN ORAL HISTORY OF SCHOOL DESEGREGATION IN FAYETTEVILLE,
ARKANSAS, 1954–1965 / JULIANNE LEWIS ADAMS, THOMAS DeBLACK; WITH AN INTRO-
DUCTION BY WILLARD GATEWOOD.
          P.   CM.
    INCLUDES BIBLIOGRAPHICAL REFERENCES AND INDEX.
    ISBN 1-55728-358-3 (CLOTH). —ISBN 1-55728-359-1 (PAPER)
    1. SCHOOL INTEGRATION—ARKANSAS—FAYETTEVILLE—HISTORY. I. DeBLACK,
THOMAS, 1951–   . II. TITLE.
    LC214.23.F39A33 1994
    370.19'344'0976714—DC20   94-17831
                                                                        CIP

CONTENTS

FOREWORD

Among the many changes that have occurred in our country in the last forty years, few, if any, have been more significant than those heralded by the Supreme Court's decision in the *Brown* case in 1954. By declaring racially segregated public schools unconstitutional, the court set in motion forces that resulted in the dismantling of the legal structure of Jim Crowism. The impact of the *Brown* decision was, of course, national in scope, but in no other region was its impact more far-reaching and traumatic than in the South. In Arkansas, as in other Southern states, racial segregation was not merely a well-established way of life, it was firmly embedded in law.

This was the South and the Arkansas in which I was born and grew up—a society that is alien to my children but about which they are curious. In fact, it was the interest manifested by my daughter, Julianne Lewis Adams, in the "civil rights revolution" that prompted me to reflect on the events surrounding school integration in my hometown of Fayetteville, Arkansas—events in which I participated as a sophomore in the local high school when it admitted the first black students.

While school desegregation generated much noise and no little violence elsewhere in the South, my hometown confronted the issue and resolved it with a good deal of dignity and grace. This is not to suggest that all residents of Fayetteville suddenly shed their racial prejudice or that all agreed on questions of strategy and timing. Rather, it is to suggest that the determination to obey the law of the land was sufficiently strong and widespread to mute such prejudice. For many, if not most, of the town's citizens, their belief in freedom, equality, and other concepts articulated by the Founding Fathers took priority over their commitment to, and acquiescence in, a school system that so patently discriminated against a particular racial group.

Furthermore, the fact that the local school board decided to integrate the high school within a matter of days after the *Brown* decision and followed through on a plan to complete the process at lower levels suggests the crucial significance of strong, competent, and responsible leadership in achieving difficult but essential social goals. Although much remains to be accomplished in the whole area of racial and ethnic relations, the school board's decision in 1954 was an important first step—a step worthy of being recorded for future generations as they, too, have to resolve problems arising from the replacement of old ways by new ones.

I am grateful for the questions directed to me by my daughter, Julianne. Her inquiries prodded me to reflect on the meaning and significance of the desegregation process in a small Southern city; a process that, for a variety of reasons explained in the following pages, stood in sharp contrast to that which occurred in the state's capital city. The process by which Fayetteville implemented school integration reveals much about the basic character of the town and its citizens, who have traditionally placed a premium on education and often dared to challenge the status quo. Such traits are all the more essential in a rapidly changing world in which future generations will confront a host of incredibly complex problems. Even though such problems may well not be of their creation, it will be essential that they solve them. Not the least of those problems will revolve around the question of how to create a society in which all races and cultures can coexist in an atmosphere of mutual civility, harmony, and peace, with each recognizing the worth and respecting the dignity of the other. The quest for such a society will undoubtedly prompt scoffs from those who dismiss it as quixotic, but failure to pursue the quest will surely compound the distress and agony of the human family. It is my hope that these pages, which focus on events in one small community as its citizens confronted the racial integration of its schools, will provide some illumination for their children and grandchildren who will be called upon to wrestle with similar, but even more complicated, issues.

John Lewis

PREFACE

In 1954 the United States Supreme Court's decision in the case of *Brown v. Board of Education* declared racially segregated schools unconstitutional. For a decade and a half thereafter, the reaction of the South to the court's mandate to rid the region of its time-honored pattern of separate but unequal schools for blacks and whites ranged from violent opposition to peaceful acquiescence. The crisis that developed in Little Rock over the integration of its Central High School in 1957 gained widespread notoriety for Arkansas as a hotbed of white racism and a leader in the phenomenon known as "massive resistance," a strategy to thwart the aims of the "second Reconstruction." Certainly no previous incident in the history of Arkansas had attracted such sustained attention or so profoundly influenced the popular image of the state.

Most of the historical literature devoted to the South's response to the *Brown* decision and the broader assault on Jim Crowism that followed in its wake has focused on larger cities in the region such as Little Rock, Birmingham, Greensboro, Montgomery, and New Orleans. Few studies have been concerned with smaller communities such as Fayetteville, Arkansas, whose response to school integration was vastly different from the course pursued by Little Rock. Because the Fayetteville experience is a part of the Southern response to the *Brown* decision and because it offers rich insight into the process by which desegregation occurred in a small city, we attempt in this work to collect and preserve the memories of those involved in that process. As would be expected, the recollections recorded here reveal a wide variety of perspectives and therefore provide different interpretations of events related to school desegregation in Fayetteville.

We are indebted to numerous people for assistance in this project. First and foremost among them is John Lewis, a native of

Fayetteville, who as a student at the local high school observed desegregation in progress. It was he who initially suggested that the story of the community's experience in responding to and implementing the *Brown* decision was not only unusual but also worthy of being preserved in written form. Closely associated with the project from its inception, Lewis not only assisted in identifying persons who, in one capacity or another, had participated in the drama of desegregation, but he also helped in scheduling interviews and secured the financial support necessary for completing the project. We are deeply indebted to the Happy Hollow Foundation and the Bank of Fayetteville for providing such support.

We owe a special debt of gratitude to all those who consented to be interviewed, took the time to review the transcriptions, and agreed to the publication of their recollections of events that significantly altered racial patterns in Fayetteville. We appreciate their candor, their tolerance of tape-recorder failures, and their graciousness in receiving us. Unfortunately, we were not able to interview all of those involved in the desegregation process, but we have attempted to include here the recollections of a cross section of school board members, school administrators and teachers, students, and citizens of the community who, either as individuals or as members of organizations, were involved in the desegregation of Fayetteville's schools. The result is a collection of interviews, conducted in 1992–93, which provide widely different perspectives and explanations not merely of the school desegregation process, but of the integration of other public facilities as well. While there was general agreement on some aspects of the process, the interviewees substantially disagreed on others. Their recollections of events associated with school integration also revealed a wide variety of emphases and what different individuals considered to be of primary importance.

We also appreciate the contributions of Dr. Winston Simpson and his staff for making available school board minutes; Andrea Cantrell and her associates in the Special Collections department of Mullins Library at the University of Arkansas, Fayetteville, who identified and made available relevant manuscript materials; and Fayetteville High School faculty, especially Susan Colvin, Susie Brooks Stewart, and Barbara Stripling, who uncovered important documents in the school library. Jeanie Wyant and Mary Kirkpatrick performed invaluable services in transcribing, typing, and editing the interviews. The Department of History of the University of Arkansas, Fayetteville, made many contributions to this project. Gary Shepard skillfully transformed poor quality photographs and negatives into suitable form for inclusion in this work.

It is our hope that this collection of reminiscences will contribute to and make easier the task of those who later undertake writing a definitive history of school desegregation in Arkansas and the South.

INTRODUCTION

SCHOOL DESEGREGATION IN FAYETTEVILLE: A FORTY-YEAR PERSPECTIVE

Willard B. Gatewood

On September 11, 1954, stories regarding the admission of black students to the previously all-white public high school in Fayetteville, Arkansas, appeared in newspapers around the country. At the opening of the fall term on the previous day, five black students entered Fayetteville High School; two more enrolled a few days later. According to a wire service news story, Fayetteville was "the first city in the Confederate South" to "break the segregation tradition following a U.S. Supreme Court ruling."[1] The ruling referred to the court's far-reaching decision in the case of *Brown v. Board of Education of Topeka, Kansas* of May 17, 1954, which overturned the "separate but equal doctrine" of 1896 and declared as inherently unequal separate schools for blacks and whites.

For more than a decade following the *Brown* decision, school districts in the South employed a variety of strategies to circumvent the court's ruling. Efforts to bring about the racial integration of Central High School in Little Rock, Arkansas, provoked a bitter and acrimonious struggle that received international attention. The so-called Little Rock crisis[2] obscured developments in school desegregation elsewhere in the state, which in some instances contrasted sharply with those in the capital city. Especially dramatic was the contrast between the responses to the *Brown* decision by the school districts in Little Rock and Fayetteville.

When the court handed down its decision, racial segregation prevailed in the schools as well as in the institutional life generally throughout the South. In Arkansas racially separate schools were

statutory rather than constitutional. The state's constitution, ratified
in 1874, merely provided for free public schools and vested in the
legislature the power to designate supervisory officers. The legislative statute that placed the management of local schools in indepen-
dent school districts required each district "to establish separate
schools for white and colored persons." In 1954 Arkansas had 423
school districts, of which 184 had no black students. The state had
1,450 white schools and 634 black schools. The average expenditure
per pupil was $102.25 for whites and $67.75 for blacks. Despite
official rhetoric about providing "separate but equal" education for
both races, schools for blacks were patently unequal to those for
whites. At the time of the *Brown* decision, no cases seeking the end
of segregated schools in Arkansas were pending in federal courts,
but petitions were on file with several school boards charging that
black students were being denied equal educational opportunities.[3]

Within the context of the segregated society that existed throughout Arkansas, both Fayetteville and Little Rock possessed reputations
for enlightened racial policies and practices. That their responses to
school desegregation in the mid-1950s took such radically different
paths resulted in large part from differences in local conditions,
especially in regard to the size of the black population, the role
assumed by community leaders, economic considerations, and the
influences of geography and historical experience.

Located on the Arkansas River near the center of the state, Little
Rock was the only city in Arkansas worthy of being classified as
an urban center. Its proximity to the plantation region to its east
and south, where the overwhelming majority of African Americans
lived, meant that the city possessed a large black population—
23,559 blacks (non-whites) out of a total of 102,213.[4] The capital city,
linked economically to the region's cotton culture, also partook gen-
erously of the values and traditions associated with the Deep South.
Regardless of the part played by cultural factors and the racial com-
position of the city's population in influencing Little Rock's response
to the *Brown* decision, the vacillation of the community's traditional
leadership appears to have been of primary significance. Whether
out of fear of the economic consequences of involvement in desegregation or because they were closet racists who secretly agreed with
Gov. Orval E. Faubus's segregationist stance, the city's establishment
refused to pursue a resolute course that would encourage the rapid
and peaceful integration of local schools.[5]

The two hundred miles between Little Rock and Fayetteville scarcely provided an accurate measure of the distance that separated the cultures each represented. Located in the Ozark Mountains in the northwest corner of Arkansas, Fayetteville was the seat of Washington County and served as a trading center for a prosperous agricultural region. Originally populated mainly by people from Tennessee, the Carolinas, and other southern states who carved out small farms and apple orchards in the valleys and on the hillsides, the vicinity around Fayetteville stood in sharp contrast to the plantation country in eastern Arkansas. Few blacks, slave or free, lived in northwest Arkansas in the antebellum era. At the outbreak of the Civil War, pro-Union sentiment was strong in the area, which in the postwar period provided substantial and persistent support for the Republican Party. The commitment to education by citizens in northwest Arkansas was evident in the existence of schools and academies throughout the area. In 1872 Fayetteville outbid all other towns in the competition for the state university. The presence of the University of Arkansas in Fayetteville was an important influence on the character of the town.[6]

The slow but steady growth of Fayetteville accelerated in the decade following the end of World War II. For the first time the University's enrollment exceeded five thousand students. Poultry and wood products had emerged as major industries in the area. In addition to the Frisco Railroad and curving mountainous highways which linked Fayetteville to the outside world, Scheduled Skyways began operation in the postwar era, and in December 1954 Central Airlines inaugurated regular service with six flights daily. Two years earlier the city opened a new, commodious high school facility for whites.[7]

Fayetteville's population in the 1950s was overwhelmingly white. Out of a population of eighteen thousand, about four hundred were African Americans. The black population resided in a section commonly known as "Tin Cup," located east of the county courthouse. Fayetteville blacks were primarily employed in the service trades, especially as domestics, cooks, and custodians. Some black veterans who returned home to Fayetteville after the war and who had acquired specialized training in the armed forces took advantage of the G.I. Bill to further improve their vocational skills. Some were able to advance up the occupational ladder, especially in the automotive service trades. A few black women also secured training that improved their job skills but were often unable to gain employment based on their newly acquired qualifications.[8]

Black education in Fayetteville began with the establishment in 1866 of a school, known as Henderson School, by the American Missionary Association, a northern philanthropic organization dedicated to the uplift of newly freed slaves. Even after the local school board assumed responsibility for black education, Henderson School continued to serve the black community despite the fact that it was located in a predominantly white neighborhood as a result of changes in the town's residential patterns. In 1934 the Civil Works Administration, a New Deal agency, hired fifteen black men to demolish an old all-white school and transport the materials to Tin Cup. These materials were used to construct Lincoln School, which was completed in 1936 by another New Deal agency, the Works Progress Administration. Lincoln School served the black community for a generation, from 1936 to 1965.[9]

Although Fayetteville provided public elementary and secondary schools for whites, it operated only a single school through the ninth grade for blacks and made no provision for their education beyond that grade for many years. Not until 1947 did the town's school board begin paying tuition, room, and board costs for those black students who wished to attend high school. The board worked out arrangements with Fort Smith, sixty miles away, and later with Hot Springs, two hundred miles away, for accommodating its black high school students.[10] Such an arrangement was in effect when the Supreme Court rendered its decision in 1954.

Despite its small size, the black population in Fayetteville had created a viable community. In addition to a school and two churches, one Baptist and the other Methodist, the community possessed several fraternal orders. A black correspondent familiar with Fayetteville's African-American community spoke about it in glowing terms in 1893. He reported that its residents were "generally prosperous and thrifty, a majority of whom own their own homes in which happiness and independence are conspicuously blended." Blacks, he pointed out, lived in safety, exercised their right to vote without fear of intimidation, and were guaranteed fair trials. Convinced that Fayetteville whites were "not as bloodthirsty as southerners are generally supposed to be," he was certain that there existed no other town "south of Mason and Dixon's line where the two races are getting along better and the Negro is afforded fairer play."[11] Although this account obviously contained exaggerations, the writer's principal point was that compared to other towns in Arkansas, especially those in the eastern and southern portions of the state, Fayetteville's blacks often did escape the grosser forms of racism.

A majority of the white residents of Fayetteville undoubtedly considered themselves Southerners and subscribed to the mores and values, racial and otherwise, associated with the region. The community's white leadership practiced a form of genteel paternalism toward its black residents within a strictly segregated society. African Americans in the town may well have had little fear of lynching and other forms of physical violence as the writer in 1893 maintained, but they scarcely enjoyed the blissful existence he described. As elsewhere in the state, the poll tax acted as a deterrent to voting by blacks and indeed by a large proportion of the town's poorer whites. Except for several ministers, one or two small entrepreneurs, and especially Lincoln School teachers, Fayetteville's black community in the 1950s lacked a middle class as usually defined in terms of income, occupation, and education. Even if Fayetteville's black population had been substantially larger, its access to political power and decision making would undoubtedly have remained extremely limited.[12]

Nevertheless, several factors helped to differentiate Fayetteville from the typical small town in Arkansas, factors which blended to shape an environment that helps explain the town's quick and positive response to the *Brown* decision in 1954. First, the small size and stability of Fayetteville's black population made it possible for whites and blacks to know each other as individuals and to keep the lines of interracial communication open. Second, the presence of the state university in the town contributed significantly to its response to the prospect of racially desegregated schools. The University of Arkansas was the first such institution in the South after Reconstruction to admit African Americans. Following the admission of Silas Hunt without any litigation to its school of law in 1948, a few black students enrolled in various professional and graduate programs.[13] By 1954 the townspeople of Fayetteville had grown accustomed to a limited degree of racial desegregation in their midst. In addition, the University faculty included a substantial number of individuals reared and educated outside the South and native Southerners with advanced degrees from non-Southern institutions, who gave expression to attitudes and values that made Fayetteville more cosmopolitan and racially tolerant than many towns of comparable size in the state. Fully aware of the increasing assaults on Jim Crowism in the post–World War II years and deeply concerned about the racial discrimination practiced in their town, individual faculty members assumed conspicuous roles in the civic life of the community and figured significantly in efforts to improve the quality of local public schools. Such involvement undoubtedly dramatized for them the gulf that existed between black and white education and strengthened their desire to eliminate such blatant inequities.[14] Finally, in the 1950s, the business leadership in Fayetteville exhibited a degree of pragmatic enlightenment that often did not exist in other parts of Arkansas. Committed to the economic development of the town and region, local business people focused much energy on enhancing the town's water supply and transportation facilities. But they were keenly interested in education and saw the link between good schools and economic development, themes pursued regularly in the *Northwest Arkansas Times,* the local newspaper owned by the family of Sen. J. William Fulbright. Proud of the town's reputation for progressivism and abreast of court actions affecting various forms of racial segregation, business leaders were intent on preventing anything likely to tarnish the town's image and thereby jeopardize its economic development. A confrontation over school desegregation, therefore, posed risks which spokesmen for the business community were not willing to take.[15]

The Fayetteville school board in 1954 consisted of six prominent and highly respected businessmen. The chairman, Ray Adams, was a florist, and the secretary, Hal C. Douglas, was Senator Fulbright's brother-in-law, publisher of the *Northwest Arkansas Times,* and general manager of the Fulbright family's diverse enterprises. The other members were Clark McClinton, owner of a highway construction company; Henry Shreve, manager of the local Campbell Soup Company operation; William C. Morton, owner of an insurance agency; and Haskell Utley, a real estate broker.[16] Fully apprised of the existence and progress of cases in the federal courts involving school desegregation, the board members were scarcely caught by surprise when the Supreme Court rendered the *Brown* decision. Although minutes of board meetings were extraordinarily brief and recorded only board actions, it seems safe to assume that the school superintendent, Virgil Blossom, and his successor, Wayne White, at least informally discussed with board members possible outcomes of pending school desegregation suits. On at least one occasion, the board considered a letter from a prominent Fayetteville physician and his wife, both "members of old southern families," who advocated the admission of black students to the all-white high school.[17] Superintendent White later reported that while no blacks "ever agitated" for school desegregation, a group of white citizens had already "hired a lawyer to bring about integration" when the school board announced its decision to integrate the high school.[18] Whatever previous discussions had taken place or the extent of pressure applied on behalf of desegregation, the Fayetteville school board voted unanimously on May 21, 1954, four days after the *Brown* decision, to integrate Fayetteville Senior High School (grades ten, eleven, and twelve) at the beginning of the fall term.[19] The *Arkansas State Press*, a black weekly published in Little Rock by L. C. and Daisy Bates, observed that the board's action could lead to the assumption "that all the brains and law-abiding white people of Arkansas live in Fayetteville."[20]

The dispatch with which the board acted does not imply that its members were uniformly enthusiastic about desegregation. Some may even have been reluctant to take such a drastic step; one or two who considered the issue within a moral context had serious misgivings about a dual system in which the school for blacks was so patently inferior. The grounds on which all agreed were expressed by Hal Douglas, who declared that the court had spoken and Fayetteville would obey "the law of the land." All board members also agreed that the desegregation of schools should take place, insofar as possible, without fanfare or publicity. The local newspaper published a story about the board's decision, and its intention, "if all went well," to integrate the junior high school grades, one per year, beginning with the ninth grade in 1955, the eighth in 1956, and the seventh in 1957. In announcing its decision to desegregate the senior high school, the board emphasized that because of "serious overcrowding" in the elementary and junior high schools, integration of these grades "must of necessity proceed more slowly."[21] Beyond the story about the board's initial decision, the *Northwest Arkansas Times* omitted comment on the local desegregation plan until the opening of the fall school term almost three months later.

Another consideration that figured significantly in the board's decision and that undoubtedly made it more palatable to some residents was the financial straits in which the Fayetteville school system found itself as the 1953–54 school year ended. The schools had a balance of "only $159 in the bank" at the close of the year. One reason for the tight budgetary situation was the spiraling costs of sending black high school students to Fort Smith and Hot Springs. Such costs amounted to five thousand dollars in 1953–54. A segregated school system, the superintendent admitted, "was a luxury" that the district "could no longer afford." Furthermore, Fort Smith had informed Fayetteville officials that because of overcrowded conditions its black high school could no longer accept out-of-town students. According to one Fayetteville school board member, the *Brown* decision "pulled us out of a hole."[22]

With virtually no publicity, efforts got underway during the late spring and summer of 1954 to insure that all "would go well." Youth organizations in various white churches explored race relations topics and met together with black youth on occasion under the auspices of the United Christian Youth Movement. One participant observed that these church-related activities "helped destroy the feeling that Negroes would not be welcome in the high school." No less important was the role of the Fayetteville chapter of United Church Women, a predominantly white group, which for some years prior to 1954 had included black women. The so-called mainline denominations, especially the Methodist, Presbyterian, Episcopal, and Christian (Disciples of Christ) congregations, were actively involved in preparing Fayetteville's white youth to transcend traditional racial mores and practices.[23]

All other preparations for the opening of schools early in September 1954 paled beside those undertaken by the principals of the schools involved in the initial integration process: Louise Bell, the principal of Fayetteville's Senior High School since 1945, and Minnie B. Dawkins, principal of Lincoln School since 1946. The two women, one white, one black, respected each other and cooperated closely to insure that desegregation would go smoothly. Mrs. Bell marshaled the high school faculty, worked with student leaders, and sponsored a tour of the facility for the black students before registration day. All the while, Miss Dawkins counseled black students who were scheduled to enter the high school and conferred with parents and others to allay their anxieties. Both women apparently agreed with the school board's position that the absence of publicity would enhance the possibility of an orderly school opening.[24]

The absence of publicity obviously worked as planned. Negative reaction to the decision to desegregate the high school appears to have been minimal. The superintendent and school board members received about a hundred letters in regard to the decision, and those in favor outnumbered those opposed by a margin of seven to one. Superintendent White reported that of the numerous townspeople who had discussed the matter personally with him, only four had been "bitter against the decision to integrate."[25] Public reaction is at best difficult to measure and hence to analyze. But available evidence suggests that a majority of residents generally agreed with the school board's position that the highest court in the nation had spoken and the only viable option was to obey its mandate. In a letter written four years later, after the political leadership of Arkansas had responded to the court's rulings with a strategy known as "massive resistance," a Fayetteville elementary school teacher provided insight into her own feelings:

> Personally, I carry a lot of the racial prejudice that most people of the South have built up over the years. I wouldn't be just tickled pink to have Negroes in my classroom, but if they were there, I would try to uphold my duties and obligations as an American citizen and teach them along with white students to the best of my ability.
>
> Let's not forget nor ignore the law of the land, the Constitution of the United States. Can't we remember, too, that whatever the color of their skin today, they are the hope of America. Let's give them a fair chance![26]

No doubt many residents of Fayetteville harbored "a lot of racial prejudice," but, like the teacher, concluded that obedience to the "law of the land" and to their sense of fairness necessitated acquiescence in school desegregation. Although school board members occasionally received hostile telephone calls, no organized protest materialized.[27]

When Fayetteville's schools opened in September 1954, black students enrolled at the senior high school without incident. The Associated Press representative present on opening day, who obviously anticipated a confrontation, canceled his order for wire photo equipment when the school year began without any unusual occurrences. A lone woman holding a placard stood across the street from the high school on opening day. Students ignored her and no one can recall the message on her placard.[28]

Stories about the integration of Fayetteville's high school appeared

prominently in many newspapers, including the *Nippon Times,*
Japan's leading English language paper. A former teacher in the
Fayetteville school system who was teaching English in a missionary
school in Tokyo in 1954 wrote home that the article in the *Nippon
Times* would "do untold good." "It quietly and simply tells a nation
of very intelligent people," she declared, "that we *do* at times practice what we preach as Christians, as educators, and as lovers of
freedom."[29]

The spirit of acceptance and friendliness exhibited by a vast
majority of the five hundred white students quickly dissipated
much of the apprehensiveness of the seven black students. That
"things went so smoothly" owed much to the roles played by the
principal, Louise Bell, and by the 26 Club, a student leadership
group. A fair-minded but strict disciplinarian, Mrs. Bell involved
students in the planning of school activities, but everyone was fully
aware that she did not tolerate what she considered unbecoming
behavior, especially any overt actions by white students designed to
torment or feed the apprehensions of their black peers. The members of the 26 Club, having been counseled during the summer on
appropriate behavior, proved to be critical in putting the black students at ease by greeting and talking to them and by welcoming
them into extracurricular activities. Because the club consisted of
student leaders, other white students tended to follow their example.
This is not to suggest the absence of racist behavior and remarks.[30]

While the initial step toward the desegregation of Fayetteville's
schools represented an example of what has been termed "quiet
change,"[31] the response to the *Brown* decision elsewhere in Arkansas
and the South prompted bitter and protracted controversy.
Various groups opposed to desegregation, such as White America,
Incorporated, and the White Citizens Councils, mounted cam-
paigns to maintain the racial status quo. Beginning in 1955, the state
legislature entered the anti-desegregation fray, largely at the urging
of members from eastern Arkansas, by seeking legislation to per-
petuate school segregation. During the three years after 1954, Gov.
Orval E. Faubus, a native of the Ozarks and originally classified as a
moderate on racial affairs, drifted into the pro-segregationist orbit
and ultimately became the national symbol of white resistance to
school desegregation. His use of the Arkansas National Guard to
block the desegregation of Little Rock's Central High School in
September 1957 precipitated a collision between state and federal

authorities that attracted international publicity.[32] By 1958, according to the *Arkansas Gazette,* the state's preeminent newspaper,
Little Rock had "become the world-wide symbol of race violence."[33]

The forces of segregation in Arkansas encountered persistent
opposition from those determined to abide by the court's desegregation mandate. Litigation instituted by the National Association
for the Advancement of Colored People attempted to integrate
Little Rock schools and to nullify the legislative stratagems enacted
to maintain segregation. Various statewide church organizations,
especially those affiliated with Presbyterian and Disciples of Christ
denominations and the interdenominational United Church Women,
lent significant support to the movement for desegregation. The
revival of the Arkansas affiliate of the Southern Regional Council,
known as the Arkansas Council on Human Relations, in March 1955
brought another interracial organization into the struggle on the side
of those seeking immediate implementation of the *Brown* decision.[34]

Most of Fayetteville's community leaders voiced opposition to
the actions of Faubus and the legislature in 1957 and 1958. For many,
the Little Rock imbroglio, publicized nationally and internationally
in both words and photographs, was a source of profound embar-
rassment, even shame. In their view, it nullified efforts to overcome
the image of Arkansas as a place inhabited by ignorant people and
Gothic politicians. Little Rock in 1957–58 appeared to confirm for
outsiders the validity of H. L. Mencken's outrageous description of
the state a generation earlier.[35] A Fayetteville couple touring Europe
late in the 1950s encountered so many inquiries from those appalled
by what they read about Little Rock that when questioned about
their place of residence in the United States they responded by saying they lived "near Texas."[36]

The *Northwest Arkansas Times* characterized the confrontation in
Little Rock over the desegregation of Central High School as serving
"no good purpose." It was "not our way" of resolving problems. The
Times was certain that the whole episode would "depress the atmosphere built carefully over a long period to attract industry" to the
state. Others in Fayetteville, notably clergymen, were even less cir-
cumspect in denouncing Governor Faubus.[37] "In other states . . .,"
Walter L. Johnson of University Baptist Church declared, "the governors have called out troops to maintain the highest law in the
land concerning integration of the races: in Arkansas a new thing

has occurred, for Governor Orval Faubus who swore to uphold the laws of the nation has called out troops to keep the highest law of the land from being obeyed."[38] Scarcely less pointed was the reference to the Arkansas governor by E. E. Thwaites of the First Presbyterian Church as a man who possessed "no respect for the laws of the nation or more important the law of God."[39] Governor Faubus singled out Presbyterian ministers for special rebuke, claiming that they had been "effectively brainwashed" by "Communists and left-wingers."[40]

Like other segregationist spokesmen, Faubus capitalized on the anti-Communist hysteria and paranoia existing in the 1950s largely as a result of Sen. Joseph McCarthy's free-wheeling crusade. References to racial integration as a part of a Communist conspiracy to undermine or destroy time-honored conventions became important weapons in the segregationists' arsenal. Not merely Presbyterian clergymen, but anyone who spoke out against segregation, risked being tagged a Communist or Communist sympathizer. At the height of "massive resistance" to desegregation, as exemplified by the rhetoric and actions of Faubus, anti-Communism and anti-integrationism became mutually supportive movements. That Faubus resorted to the use of the loyalty issue against his opponents was all the more ironic in view of the fact that he himself had been the target of such smear tactics in his initial campaign for governor in 1954.[41]

The polarization of opinion, dramatized by the struggle over desegregation waged by contending forces and by the climatic events surrounding Little Rock's Central High School, was not without impact on the situation in Fayetteville. As early as October 4, 1954, the town's *Northwest Arkansas Times* insisted that school desegregation was "no reason for disorder." While citizens had a right to voice their opposition to the court's decision, it argued, "the only right they have of protest is an orderly one." But the *Times* maintained that any attack on school children involved in desegregation was "highly improper" and that anyone "who raises his hand against the boys and girls deserved whatever the courts of the country can give him." A recurring editorial theme in the *Times* was the insistence on orderly desegregation and the avoidance of violence which insured that "nobody gains."[42]

Letters to the editor in the newspaper indicated that Fayetteville did not escape the polarization of opinion evident throughout the state: on the one hand, were communications from those who believed that school desegregation would "lead to intermarriage and the ultimate mongrelization of the white race;" on the other, were letters which argued that segregation was morally and legally wrong, as well as expensive, and was "favored by only a small minority" of Fayetteville's population. The historical evidence does indeed indicate that only a "small minority" publicly opposed school desegregation. With the exception of a retired army officer who, quick to denounce any proposed change as "radical," applauded the White Citizens Councils, the opposition was rarely vocal and was scattered rather than organized in Fayetteville.[43]

While the debate intensified, the town's desegregation plan continued on schedule at the opening of school in the fall of 1955 with the incorporation of ninth grade black students into previously all-white schools. The principal impact of the agitation was on the high school's athletic program, especially its football schedule. Fayetteville was a town which took football seriously, so any tampering with the football schedule was a matter of grave concern. On October 13, 1955, J. M. ("Johnnie") Burnett, the executive secretary of the Arkansas Athletic Association (AAA), announced that the organization's executive committee had adopted a policy making blacks ineligible to participate in athletic contests with all-white teams without prior agreement between the schools represented. The problem arose when Fort Smith and Russellville canceled games scheduled with Fayetteville because the latter had blacks on its football team. One such player was William ("Bull") Hayes, an outstanding athlete who was universally popular with the entire student body.[44] Harry Vandergriff, Fayetteville High's football coach since 1949, who strongly objected to the AAA policy, called together his team to determine its reaction. The team voted unanimously to forego playing any team which objected to its black members. The school board endorsed the position taken by Coach Vandergriff and his team and decided "that in the future all high school activities should be on an integrated basis." As a result, the high school athletic teams thereafter had to schedule games with schools in Missouri or those in Arkansas such as Siloam Springs, which agreed in advance to play a racially integrated team. The approach of Coach Vandergriff and the actions of his teams, fully supported by the school board, contributed significantly to the success of school desegregation.[45]

In September 1957, while the crisis at Little Rock's Central High

School dominated the headlines, Fayetteville completed the integration of its junior high school grades. But the atmosphere throughout Arkansas became increasingly tense in the wake of the Little Rock crisis and the events that occurred in its aftermath. The enactment of a series of anti-integration laws by the legislature, Governor Faubus's closing of the Little Rock schools in 1958, and a succession of dramatic courtroom maneuvers combined to create a "war of nerves." The Fayetteville school board was aware of the sweeping powers over public education bestowed on Governor Faubus by the special session of the legislature in August, 1958. So broad were the powers that the governor could presumably close any public school in the state "at his pleasure." That he used this legislation to close the Little Rock schools was not lost on those in charge of Fayetteville's schools.[46]

Never far from the mind of Fayetteville's political spokesmen was the welfare of the University of Arkansas, which, dependent on legislative appropriations, was of major significance to the health of the Fayetteville economy. Some concluded that to alienate the governor and the legislature that he controlled by flying in the face of his segregationist position was to jeopardize university appropriations. But two members of the legislature from Fayetteville, Rep. Charles Stewart and Sen. Clifton ("Deacon") Wade, opposed the passage of the law, known as Act 10. Enacted by the special legislative session of 1958, the measure required that, as a condition of employment, every teacher in a state-supported school, including the University of Arkansas, must sign an affidavit listing every organization to which he or she had belonged and regularly contributed during the previous five years. Although the act was aimed primarily at teachers who were members or contributors to the NAACP, segregationists by their own admission intended to use it to "rid the state of Communist instructors," as well as school personnel who belonged to the American Civil Liberties Union, American Association of University Professors, Urban League, and other organizations that supported school desegregation. The trustees and faculty of the University vigorously protested Act 10, as did the *Northwest Arkansas Times,* which in 1957 had opposed a similar "loyalty oath" bill that was ultimately withdrawn. Such legislation, the *Times* concluded, threatened the "liberty of us all" by establishing a "police state."[47]

Local considerations, as well as uncertainties created by recently enacted legislation and pending litigation concerning public schools, undoubtedly figured in the decision to postpone the integration of Fayetteville's elementary schools. Aside from the problem of over-crowding, the school board was well aware that not all blacks were enthusiastic about integrating the elementary grades and closing Lincoln School.[48] While few actively opposed such a course, some black parents had misgivings about sending their children to schools located at considerably greater distances from home than Lincoln and about potential problems in their adjustment to the predomi-nantly white environment that they would encounter. Whatever its reasons, the Fayetteville school board took no steps to extend deseg-regation to the black elementary students at Lincoln School once the junior and senior high schools had been integrated in 1957.

The continued postponement of action regarding Lincoln School exhausted the patience of those anxious to complete school desegre-gation. The result was a movement by organizations and individuals to prod the school board to act. One such organization was the Fayetteville Community Relations Association, an interracial group established around 1960, which concerned itself "with improving various aspects of race relations in the Fayetteville community." The Association ultimately included 280 members, but its executive committee, known as the Council, actually did most of the work. The Council not only conducted workshops, made studies of the local racial environment, circulated petitions, and published a newsletter, but more important, the organization also provided a vehicle through which local blacks could become actors in, rather than mere observers of, a drama that so directly affected them. Among whites actively involved in the Council were Keith Peterson, a professor of political science at the University of Arkansas, Lyell Thompson, a professor of agriculture, and Philip Bashor, a profes-sor of philosophy, and his wife, Lorraine Bashor. Three blacks, Minerva Carroll, Lodene Deffebaugh, and Carlos Carr, also figured prominently in the activities of the Council. Although the Council was concerned with employment opportunities, housing, and other issues affecting Fayetteville's black citizens, it took particular inter-est in the integration of the town's elementary schools. Because the Council concluded that the inadequate preparation of black students at Lincoln accounted for their high drop-out rate in the integrated junior and senior high grades, it pressed the school board to move toward the elimination of the sole remaining segre-gated all-black school.[49] "The continued existence of Lincoln School as a separate (and unequal) all-Negro facility," Peterson declared, "is indefensible on various grounds, among other things it is both uneconomical and illegal."[50]

Complementing the activities of the Association were those of the Fayetteville chapter of the League of Women Voters (LWV). In fact, the two organizations cooperated on the matter of eliminating the segregated, all-black Lincoln School. In the fall of 1963, the League adopted as its primary project "The Study and Support of Adequate Education for All Children in the Fayetteville School District." From its study, the LWV decided that the Lincoln School issue took priority over its other educational concerns. The League recommended: "(1) The children of Lincoln School, the segregated Negro Elementary School, should be integrated by the fall of 1964. (2) All Negro children should be sent to the elementary school nearest their home, not distributed among elementary schools of the city."[51] Under the leadership of Dr. Wilma Sacks, a well-known physician, Mrs. LeMon Clark, the wife of a physician, and other women prominent in the civic life of Fayetteville, the League presented its findings and recommendations to the school board and requested that the board open its meetings to interested citizens. Replying for the board, Superintendent White omitted any reference to open board meetings but declared that Mrs. LeMon Clark, the head of the LWV school committee, would be welcomed at all board meetings. The school board also informed the League that it had already decided to discontinue operation of Lincoln School in the fall of 1965. Board president Henry Shreve explained that it was necessary to delay the action until 1965 because of "many problems" associated with closing of Lincoln. These problems included the relocation of black teachers, disposition of the teacherage, and the proper distribution of students among the elementary schools in order to prevent overcrowding.[52]

To prepare for the transfer of black students, the League organized a six-week summer school for such students "to close the gap," both academically and culturally. The summer school, operated by volunteers, was designed to acclimate black students to working and associating with whites as well as providing them with remedial academic studies, since the League's investigation had also revealed that the separate and unequal system of education for blacks had not prepared them to perform satisfactorily. Attendance at the summer school was purely voluntary, but nearly all Lincoln students enrolled. In February 1965 the League also established and staffed a reading clinic at Lincoln School. Complementing such activities was the kindergarten for black children, which for two years League member Lorraine Bashor, who was also active in the Fayetteville Community Relations Council, had been conducting at the black St. James Church in order to prepare them to enter the first grade without disadvantages. Such a program foreshadowed the federally funded "Operation Headstart" by several years.[53]

Alongside the efforts of the Fayetteville Community Relations Association and the League of Women Voters were the less visible, behind-the-scenes activities of numerous individuals. Some worked with the Arkansas Council on Human Relations (ACHR), which attempted to promote statewide desegregation through "education, negotiation and conciliation." It organized conferences, provided speakers, and issued reports on the progress of desegregation. For example, Thelma Engler, the wife of a University of Arkansas professor and state president of United Church Women, who be-friended the first black students to attend the university, was inti-mately involved in the affairs of the ACHR.[54] Elaine McNeil, a sociologist and a specialist in race relations, labored quietly but effectively to insure that school desegregation would not only take place, but take place smoothly. McNeil and like-minded women formed the World Affairs Group, which possessed neither formal structure nor officers, but which met informally twice a month ini-tially to discuss international affairs such as nuclear war, peace and similar topics. In time, these educated, talented, and concerned women with ample leisure to pursue topics that interested them focused their attention on desegregation issues. Through the use of an ingenious strategy, the group made the efforts of their small number appear as expressions of a much larger movement.[55] In a letter to the director of ACHR early in 1957 about a recently "inte-grated Girl Scout troop" in Fayetteville, McNeil wrote: "All very quiet, and I guess it should remain so. There's a long story there too, involving the triumph of people believing in racial equality over the separate-but-equal paternalism. . . ."[56] Like McNeil and Engler, numerous others whose names rarely appeared in the media quietly sought to enhance communication between blacks and whites and to remove barriers, such as the continued existence of Lincoln School as an all-black, segregated and unequal educational institu-tion, that denied blacks equal opportunities.

Late in 1963, the year in which movie theaters in Fayetteville, as well as the municipal swimming pool, became integrated,[57] the Junior Chamber of Commerce added its endorsement to the movement to complete the school desegregation process. In December 1963 the Junior Chamber's Community Development Committee reported:

> The school board began an integrated school system in the fall of 1954 without hysteria or mere lip service to the law. Integrated schools have saved the system sorely needed dollars, improved the education for our minority racial group, and complied with the spirit and letter of the law. We feel they should and will quickly complete this program with the elimination of Lincoln School. The separate condition forced on the young children of colored Americans in this district cannot but further any feeling of separateness we may have .... Procrastination gains nothing in this area.[58]

The rising generation of Fayetteville's business leaders, by adopting this statement, threw its critically important support behind the movement to discontinue the existence of the town's remaining segregated, all-black school.

As the national movement for civil rights broadened in scope and gained momentum in the early 1960s, Fayetteville's black community became increasingly active in efforts to complete the desegregation of local schools. In addition to their participation in interracial groups, black residents formed organizations of their own, such as the Community Concerns on Equality (CCOE).[59] Individual African Americans, such as Lodene Deffebaugh, who had become president of Fayetteville's Community Relations Association, assumed the role of "warriors." Other blacks, especially Minerva Hoover, Carlos Carr, Rosetta Dowell, and Christine Childress, also assumed important roles in the movement to dismantle racial barriers in public schools, as well as in movie theaters, restaurants, and other public places in which segregation existed.[60] As the president of Lincoln School's Parent-Teacher Association, Deffebaugh galvanized the school's patrons in voicing opposition to the continued existence of segregated elementary education in Fayetteville. Deffebaugh led a group of Lincoln parents who appeared before the school board on October 30, 1963, to request the elimination of Lincoln and the integration of its students into the white elementary schools. The group again appeared before the

board on January 14, 1964, with four specific requests: (1) the closing of Lincoln School by the opening of the fall term in 1964; (2) the
integration of its students into Washington and Jefferson schools,
the two white schools nearest the black residential district; (3) the
integration of black faculty and school personnel into existing schools; (4) the "recruitment of more Negro teachers" for
Fayetteville schools. These requests had the endorsement and support of the newly formed and short-lived organization in the black
community, the CCOE, headed by J. B. Moorage. After the group of
Lincoln parents presented its recommendations, the school board,
at the same meeting on January 14, voted to discontinue Lincoln
School and to complete school desegregation "not later than
September, 1965." On several occasions thereafter, Superintendent
White and members of the school board, including Clark McClinton,
met at Lincoln School with the parents of its students to discuss
plans for completing school desegregation and to explain steps to be
taken to prepare black elementary students for integration into all-
white schools.[61]

    Some black residents continued to have misgivings about discon-
tinuing Lincoln School, misgivings encouraged by one or two individuals, especially Pearlie Williams who became principal of the
school after Minnie Dawkins joined the faculty of Philander Smith
College in Little Rock. Whatever her reasons, Ms. Williams openly
opposed the closing of Lincoln. Her activities aroused deep resentment among blacks who favored school desegregation. Their opposition to her reappointment may well account for the failure of the
school board to renew her contract at the end of the school year in
1964.[62] Opposition to the closing of Lincoln School disappeared
shortly thereafter in the black community.

    The school board's plan for discontinuing Lincoln School and
integrating its student body into the city's other elementary schools
incorporated virtually all of the recommendations made by
the League of Women Voters and other civic organizations, including the provision for black children to attend the school nearest
their residence. This provision meant that black children would
attend Washington, Jefferson, or Bates schools. On May 10, 1965,
Superintendent White announced that the United States Office of
Education had approved the school board's plan for completing the
town's school desegregation.[63] The *Northwest Arkansas Times* greeted
White's announcement with "undeniable pride" and complimented

the school board for its steady, deliberative course in the face of clamor by some "for faster action." "There is no real question on this matter," the *Times* editorialized. "Fayetteville has led Arkansas as well as the entire South on this matter [school desegregation] in thoughtful, progressive, systematic desegregation."[64] Compared with the chaos and disorder prompted by school desegregation elsewhere in Arkansas and the South, Fayetteville had indeed managed with considerable effort to stage a peaceful revolution.

Lincoln School closed at the end of the spring term in 1965, and the following fall its students entered Washington, Jefferson, and Bates schools without incident. Two of the schools' black teachers, the principal, Romey Thomason, and his wife, Thelma Thomason, were assigned to other schools in the district. The Lincoln School building, which for a generation had served not only as the educational institution for blacks, but also as a civic center of the black community, was later razed to make way for a housing project. A year before Lincoln School ceased operation, Melvin Eugene Dowell, the son of Rosetta and Henry Dowell, who was a Lincoln alumnus and a graduate of Fayetteville High School, became "the first Fayetteville Negro to graduate from the University of Arkansas."[65]

The desegregation of public schools in Fayetteville followed what has been termed a "quiet, gradual, non-violent pattern."[66] Sociologists and social psychologists have observed that confusion and perplexity invariably accompany radical alterations in "institutional patterns and group norms" such as those prompted by school desegregation. In such times communities become receptive to the influence of authorities who provide new definitions of the changed conditions and "cues for appropriate behavior." Therefore, the initial response of policy-makers to the *Brown* decision was of critical importance in determining the progress and ultimate outcome of the desegregation process: an ambiguous or inconsistent response meant that successful resistance to desegregation was probable, while a resolute response was more likely to result in desegregation.[67] The unambiguous, prompt, and positive response to the *Brown* decision by the six business and civic leaders who made up the Fayetteville school board lends credence to such observations. Careful planning by school administrators, white and black, to implement the board's clear and firm policy of desegregation substantially reduced the risk of turmoil at the opening of school in the fall of 1954.

By the time the desegregation of the senior and junior high schools had been completed, conflicting pressures exerted upon the Fayetteville school board slowed the completion of the school desegregation process. Governor Faubus's defiance of federal authority not only produced anti-integration state laws that affected all public schools in Arkansas including, of course, those in Fayetteville, but also created an environment in which the forces of segregation felt free to intimidate and threaten those intent on obeying "the law of the land." At the same time the civil rights movement assumed a new militancy and expanded far beyond school desegregation to mount assaults on all forms of legalized Jim Crowism. These developments, which brought in their wake mob action, riots, and various other eruptions of violence, meant that the Fayetteville school board encountered pressures from two conflicting sources just as it contemplated the elimination of segregated elementary education: on the one hand, it had to cope with the die-hard segregationist stand of the governor, and on the other, it confronted the demands for the immediate elimination of all vestiges of segregation. These conflicting pressures complicated the board's intention to obey the "law of the land" as did the reluctance of a few local blacks to give up Lincoln School, a black community center as well as a school located in the heart of the black residential district.

Even though the resolve displayed by the traditional community leadership of Fayetteville in responding positively to the *Brown* decision contrasted sharply to the wavering and inconsistent reaction of its counterpart in Little Rock, the experiences of the two cities in grappling with school desegregation were similar at least in one respect, namely the important role played by women. In both cities, educated, civic-minded, middle-class women applied decisive pressure at crucial junctures in the desegregation struggle. In Little Rock, the activities of the Women's Emergency Committee to Open Our Schools constituted a critically important element in the campaign that reopened the city's schools after they had been closed by Governor Faubus. In 1959 Little Rock's schools reopened and its white high schools were desegregated peacefully. In Fayetteville, the involvement of women in desegregation predated, in a few instances, the *Brown* decision, as in the case of the United Church Women. Beginning with the school board's decision to integrate schools, the role of women assumed greater significance as evidenced by the part played by Louise Bell and Minnie Dawkins in implementing the board's policy. Thereafter, a network of women, both as individ-uals and as members of organizations, including the Fayetteville Community Relations Association, Arkansas Council on Human Relations, United Church Women, League of Women Voters, and World Affairs Group, exerted influence that accelerated both school integration and the end of segregation in other public places in Fayetteville. The effectiveness of women and the organizations in which they either dominated or figured prominently owed much to their strategy: the adoption of plans of action only after careful study and extensive discussion; persistence in advocating the imple-mentation of such plans; and the avoidance of dissension and conflict among different groups through inter-organizational coordi-nation and "networking." Even while prodding school authorities to "move faster" in completing the desegregation process, women used tactics that enabled them to escape giving the appearance of assum-ing an adversarial position. They made recommendations, rather than demands, and avoided the use of provocative or belligerent language in their communications with the school board. Theirs was the tactic of persistent pressure through rational discourse—a tactic that proved to be highly effective in achieving the objective of school desegregation without the acrimony and bitterness so evi-dent in other communities.

Although eleven years elapsed between the initiation of the desegregation process and its completion in 1965, Fayetteville had accomplished in an orderly and nonviolent manner an alteration in "institutional patterns and group norms" that elsewhere spawned disorder and bequeathed a legacy of embittered race relations. Virtually all agree that two considerations in particular figured significantly in the initial decision to integrate Fayetteville schools. One was the town's small black population. As Harry S. Ashmore pointed out in 1954, even though the ratio of black to white popula-tion "is not the final determinant of racial attitudes," it is "perhaps the most powerful single influence, for the practical results of desegregation depend heavily upon it."[68] A second important factor involved in the decision to desegregate Fayetteville schools was purely economic, namely the rising costs of sending black students elsewhere to attend high school. Whatever considerations prompted Fayetteville's school policy makers to embrace desegregation so promptly after the *Brown* decision, the town's ultimate success in implementing the new policy and in altering traditional racial arrangements owed much to the school board's steadfast adherence to its initial decision, the carefully laid plans followed by school administrators and teachers, and the broad support for the concept of school desegregation by articulate, influential people in the community. In many respects, the Fayetteville experience constituted a textbook example of procedures essential to successful and peaceful school desegregation in communities in which firmly entrenched racial segregation existed.

Notes

The author is especially indebted to three colleagues, James S. Chase, Jeannie Whayne, and Randall B. Woods, and to five participants in the desegregation process, Philip and Lorrie Bashor, Lodene Deffebaugh, John Lewis, and Elaine McNeil, for their assistance in preparing this essay.

    1. *Northwest Arkansas Times* (Fayetteville), September 11, 1954; whether Fayetteville was indeed the first Arkansas school district to integrate raises an interesting point, because Charleston, a town in western Arkansas, actually integrated its schools (eleven blacks out of a total of six hundred school children) at the opening of the fall term on August 23, 1954. But the Charleston school board voted to integrate "in the summer" after holding a mass meeting at which no objections were voiced. The school board in Sheridan, a town near Little Rock, voted to integrate its schools on May 21, 1954, but rescinded the decision on the following day when whites protested. Therefore, Fayetteville would be "the Confederacy's first" school district to institute successful desegregation, if such a designation is based on the time of the school board's decision, which in the case of Fayetteville was May 21, 1954, four days after the *Brown* decision. See *Southwest American* (Fort Smith), September 11, 12, 1954; *Southern School News 1* (September 3, 1954): 2; *Arkansas Gazette* (Little Rock), May 22, 1954; *Los Angeles Times*, September 12, 15, 1954; *Orlando Sentinel*, September 12, 1954.

    2. Particularly useful among the substantial body of works devoted to the Little Rock Crisis are Numan V. Bartley, *The Rise of Massive Resistance: Race and Politics in the South During the 1950s* (Baton Rouge: Louisiana State University Press, 1969), 251–69; Elizabeth Jacoway, "Taken By Surprise: Little Rock Business Leaders and Desegregation," in *Southern Businessmen and Desegregation,* Elizabeth Jacoway and David R. Colburn, eds. (Baton Rouge: Louisiana State University Press, 1982), 15–41; Jerry Vervack, "Road to Armageddon: Arkansas and *Brown v. Board of Education,* May 17, 1954 to September 2, 1957," M.A. thesis,

University of Arkansas, Fayetteville, 1973; Daisy Bates, *The Long Shadow of Little Rock: A Memoir* (Fayetteville: University of Arkansas Press, 1987); Tony Freyer, *The Little Rock Crisis: A Constitutional Interpretation* (Westport, Conn.: Greenwood Press, 1984).

3. *Southern School News* 1 (September 3, 1954): 2.

4. Bureau of the Census, *Census of Population 1950, vol. 2, Characteristics of the Population, pt.4, Arkansas* (Washington: Government Printing Office, 1952), 50 (hereafter cited as Bureau of the Census, *Arkansas, 1950*).

5. Jacoway, "Taken By Surprise," 28.

6. See William S. Campbell, *One Hundred Years of Fayetteville, 1828–1928* (Fayetteville, Ark.: n.p., 1928); Harrison Hale, *University of Arkansas, 1871–1948* (Fayetteville: University of Arkansas Alumni Association, 1948), 10–12.

7. Data gathered from the files of Fayetteville's *Northwest Arkansas Times,* January 1, 1950–December 31, 1954, and the centennial edition of the paper, June 14, 1960.

8. Bureau of the Census, *Arkansas, 1950,* 49; Gordon D. Morgan, *Black Hillbillies of the Ozarks* (Fayetteville: Department of Sociology, University of Arkansas, 1973), 135–38; Peter Kunkel and Sara S. Kennard, *Spout Spring: A Black Community* (New York: Holt, Rinehart, and Winston, 1971), 85–87.

9. Washington County Retired Teachers Association, *School Days, School Days: The History of Education in Washington County, 1830–1850* (n.p., n.d.), 52–53; Willard B. Gatewood Jr., "Arkansas Negroes in the 1890s: Documents," *Arkansas Historical Quarterly* 33 (Winter 1974): 312; "Henderson School Built in 1868," *Northwest Arkansas Times,* July 16, 1978; "Henderson School—Then and Now," *Flashback* 28 (August 1977): 47–48; Stephen Dew, "The New Deal and Fayetteville, Arkansas, 1933–1941," M.A. thesis, University of Arkansas, Fayetteville, 1987, 65; Lessie S. Read, "Lincoln School (Colored)," Manuscript, Washington County Historical Society, Fayetteville, Arkansas.

10. Minutes of the Meeting of the Fayetteville School Board, April 1, 1974, School Administration Building, Fayetteville, Arkansas (hereafter cited as School Board Minutes); see also "Arkansas," *Southern School News* 1 (September 3, 1954): 2; *Northwest Arkansas Times,* May 22, 1954; *Arkansas Gazette,* May 23, 1954; the practice of paying expenses of black high school students to attend schools elsewhere was common in towns whose African-American population was too small to "warrant" a separate black high school.

11. Gatewood, "Arkansas Negroes in the 1890s," 311–15.

12. Kunkel and Kennard, *Spout Spring,* 85–87; Gordon Morgan and Izola Preston, "History of Black Community Interwoven With City's," *Northwest Arkansas Times,* July 16, 1978.

13. A. Stephen Stephan, "Integration and Sparse Negro Populations," *School and Society* 81 (April 1955): 133–35; Gordon D. Morgan and Izola Preston, *The Edge of the Campus: A Journal of the Black Experience at the University of Arkansas* (Fayetteville: University of Arkansas Press, 1990), 11–14; A. Stephen Stephan. "Desegregation of Higher Education in Arkansas," *Journal of Negro Education* 27 (Summer 1958): 243–59.

14. See files of *Northwest Arkansas Times,* 1950–54.

15. Ibid., September 4, 11, October 8, 1954.

16. For information on school board members, I am indebted to William C. Morton, Clark McClinton, John Lewis, and Mrs. Haskell Utley.

17. A. Stephen Stephan, "Integration in Arkansas," *The Christian Century* 71 (November 24, 1954): 1427.

18. "Arkansas," *Southern School News* 1 (October 1, 1954): 3.

19. School Board Minutes, May 21, 1954.

20. *Arkansas State Press* (Little Rock), June 18, 1954.

21. See William C. Morton interview below, pp. 47–57; *Northwest Arkansas Times,* May 22, 1954; *Arkansas Gazette,* May 23, 1954.

22. Quotations found in "Arkansas," *Southern School News* 1 (October 1, 1954): 3.

23. Stephan, "Integration in Arkansas," 1426.

24. See interviews below with Louise Bell, pp. 58–62, and John Lewis, pp. 123–30.

25. *Southern School News* 1 (September 3, 1954): 2; see also B. Long (Los Angeles) to Fayetteville High School, September ?, 1954; James M. Rogers (New Orleans) to Mrs. Bunn Bell, September 16, 1954; Paul B. Kennedy (Ontario, California) to Mrs. Louise Bell, September 20, 1954; Alfred Davis (New York City) to Mrs. Bunn Bell, October 19, 1954, Fayetteville High School Library, Fayetteville, Arkansas.

26. "Teacher," letter to the editor, *Arkansas Gazette,* August 17, 1958.

27. Stephan, "Integration in Arkansas," 1427.

28. Ibid., 1426; see interview with David McClinton below, pp. 95–96.

29. Stephan, "Integration in Arkansas," 1426.

30. Ibid.; see interviews below with Louise Bell, pp. 58–62, and John Lewis, pp. 123–30; on the 26 Club see *Northwest Arkansas Times,* March 3, 1957.

31. See Lona Benedict, "The Process of Integration in a Southern Small City," M.A. thesis, University of Arkansas, Fayetteville, 1967, 3.

32. A. Stephen Stephan and Charles A. Hicks, "Integration and Segregation in Arkansas—One Year Afterward," *Journal of Negro Education* 24 (Summer 1955): 180–84; David Wallace, "Orval Eugene Faubus, 1955–1967" in Timothy P. Donovan and Willard B. Gatewood, eds., *The Governors of Arkansas: Essays in Political Biography*

(Fayetteville: University of Arkansas Press, 1981), 217–22; Neil R. McMillan, "The White Citizens Council and Resistance to School Desegregation in Arkansas," *Arkansas Historical Quarterly* 30 (Summer 1971): 95–122; *Northwest Arkansas Times,* February 25, March 21, May 1, 17, September 3, November 7, 1956.

33. *Arkansas Gazette,* August 30, 1958.

34. Stephan, "Integration and Segregation in Arkansas," 182–83; for a valuable description and analysis of the Arkansas Council on Human Relations, see Elaine O. McNeil, "White Members of a Biracial Voluntary Association in Arkansas," Ph.D. diss., University of Kansas, 1967.

35. See files of the *New York Times* from September 1954 through August 1958, for example.

36. Information provided by Elaine O. McNeil, June 24, 1954.

37. *Northwest Arkansas Times,* September 5, 27, 1957.

38. Ibid., September 7, 1957; see also letter to the editor from Presbyterian ministers in Northwest Arkansas in ibid., September 6, 1957.

39. Ibid., June 7, 1958.

40. Ibid.

41. *Arkansas Gazette,* August 16, 27, 28, 29, 1958; in his campaign for governor in 1954, Faubus's attendance at Commonwealth College in Mena, Arkansas, had prompted charges that the institution was a hotbed of Communism. See Wallace, "Orval Eugene Faubus," 216, 218.

42. *Northwest Arkansas Times,* October 4, 1954, February 7, 1956.

43. Ibid., September 13, 14, 1957, June 10, 1958.

44. Ibid., October 24, 1955; on "Bull" Hayes, see the *Times,* October 12, 14, 15, 20, 1955.

45. See Harry Vandergriff interview, below, pp. 67–75; School Board Minutes, September 20, 1955; *Northwest Arkansas Times,* September 14, 1955.

46. *Arkansas Gazette,* August 27, 28, 29, 1958; *Northwest Arkansas Times,* August 27, September 8, 12, 13, 18, 29, 30, 1958.

47. *Arkansas Gazette,* August 28, 29, 1958; *Northwest Arkansas Times,* April 2, 1957, August 23, 1958; on Act 10, see *Acts of Arkansas, Regular Session of 1959 and Extraordinary Session of 1958* (Camden, Ark.: Hurley Co., 1959), 2018–21; Robert A. Leflar, *The First Hundred Years: The Centennial History of the University of Arkansas* (Fayetteville: University of Arkansas Foundation, 1972), 199–202.

48. A review of School Board Minutes between 1954 and 1965 reveals that crowded schools and finances were the two issues that the board repeatedly addressed.

49. Benedict, "The Process of Integration in a Southern Small City," 12; Keith Peterson to Mrs. LeMon Clark, March 16, 1964, Fayetteville Community Relations Council, "Report on Lincoln School Integration"

(1964), Washington County League of Women Voters Papers, Mullins Library, University of Arkansas, Fayetteville (hereafter cited as League of Women Voters Papers); Keith Peterson to Hal Douglas, April 15, 1964, in School Board Minutes for 1964.

50. Keith Peterson, letter to the editor, *Northwest Arkansas Times,* December 18, 1963.

51. "Desegregation of Fayetteville Schools, 1963," "Lincoln School Summer Project—1964," League of Women Voters Papers; *Northwest Arkansas Times,* March 26, 1964.

52. Wilma Sacks to Henry Shreve, January 22, 1964, Henry Shreve to Wilma Sacks, March 16, 1964, League of Women Voters Papers.

53. "Lincoln Summer School Project—1964," "Closing the Gap— Academic and Cultural," Wilma Sacks to Donald Sullivan, February 3, 1965, League of Women Voters Papers.

54. Stephen Stephan to Nat Griswold (Director of Arkansas Council on Human Relations), February 20, 1956, Thelma Engler to Nat Griswold, October 20, 1960, Keith Peterson to Nat Griswold, October 4, 1960, Nat Griswold to Keith Peterson, October 20, 1960, Nat Griswold to Keith Peterson, September 1, 1961, Arkansas Council on Human Relations Papers, Special Collections, Mullins Library, University of Arkansas, Fayetteville; see also McNeil, "White Members of a Biracial Voluntary Association in Arkansas."

55. On the World Affairs Group and their strategy, see the interview with Elaine O. McNeil below, pp. 149–57.

56. Elaine O. McNeil to Margaret and Nat Griswold, March 1, 1957, Arkansas Council on Human Relations Papers.

57. Keith Peterson to Henry Shreve, March 15, 1964, in School Board Minutes for 1964.

58. Quoted in the *Northwest Arkansas Times,* December 16, 1963.

59. J. B. Morgan to Henry Shreve, April 19, 1964, in School Board Minutes for 1964.

60. See interviews with Lodene Deffebaugh and Philip and Lorraine Bashor below, pp. 158–71.

61. School Board Minutes, October 14, 30, 1963, January 14, 1964; J. B. Morgan to Henry Shreve, April 19, 1964, in School Board Minutes for 1964.

62. Keith Peterson to Hal Douglas, April 15, 1964, in School Board Minutes for 1964; School Board Minutes, May 26, 1964; Pearlie (spelled sometimes as Pearley) Williams, who also served as housemother at Scott House, a residence provided by the University of Arkansas for black women students, regularly reported to the Arkansas State Police on the activities of black and white "integrationists." Such people were under surveillance by the police who reported to Governor Faubus. See

especially State Police reports by Lt. Howard Chandler to Governor Faubus dated October 16 and November 4, 1963, in Orval E. Faubus Papers, Mullins Library, University of Arkansas, Fayetteville.

63. *Northwest Arkansas Times,* May 10, 13, 1965; Philip Bashor, letter to the editor, ibid., May 18, 1965.

64. Ibid., May 14, 1965.

65. School Board Minutes, July 2, 1965; *Northwest Arkansas Times,* June 2, 1964.

66. See the conclusions of Benedict, "The Process of Integration in a Southern Small City."

67. Elaine O. McNeil, "Policy-Makers and the Public," *Southwestern Social Science Quarterly* 39 (September 1958): 95–99.

68. Harry S. Ashmore, *The Negro and the Schools* (Chapel Hill: University of North Carolina Press, 1954), 128.

PART ONE

PUBLIC SCHOOL

ADMINISTRATORS

AND TEACHERS

WAYNE H. WHITE

Wayne H. White, a native of Nashville, Arkansas, who was educated at the University of Arkansas in Fayetteville, served as a teacher, principal, and superintendent in various school systems in the state prior to becoming superintendent of Fayetteville schools in 1953.

INTERVIEWER: Mr. White, let me start out by asking you when you came to Fayetteville, what the situation was at the time you came.

WAYNE H. WHITE: Well, I came here in 1953. I had been superintendent of schools in Siloam Springs, and, of course, that was just before the Supreme Court decision in '54, and there was a lot of talk and a lot of speculation, and it was pretty generally understood on the school board that whenever it became legal that we would begin integration because at that time—you have the history, I suppose—of how we were sending students to Fort Smith and so on.

I: Right.

WW: So that was—but no, of course, no decision [by the Fayetteville school board] was made until after actually the decision was actually made by the Supreme Court.

I: Mr. White, how do you account for the fact that the Fayetteville school board acted so promptly in responding positively to the *Brown* decision of '54.

WW: Well, I think mainly because we anticipated it. And also, it just happened that we had a school board meeting, I believe it was five days after the Supreme Court decision, and Hal Douglas, who was on the school board and who was a brother-in-law to Senator [J. William] Fulbright, was very much aware of the situation—he brought it up at the school board meeting, at the first meeting we had after the Supreme Court decision, and said, "Well, now it's the law of the land. We ought to integrate. And we have a very good reason for doing so, having to send these students all the way down to Fort Smith for high school education." So, there was very little discussion about it. All the board members concurred. I was the only one that was dragging my feet because I was thinking about the repercussions in the rest of the state. And I was under great pressure from other superintendents not to take any action, because they knew that we might, because it wouldn't be a big problem here, but they thought that that would put a lot of pressure on them to integrate.

I: You're talking about in this area or statewide?

WW: Statewide, no, mostly downstate. So, I questioned whether we ought to do it right at that time, and all the board members were in unanimous agreement that it was the time to do it. It was the law of the land, and we should go ahead. It was in the best interests of the students, and so we should do what was right.

I: Had Mr. [Virgil] Blossom or had you kept the board informed about the pending litigation and the possibility that this might happen? Had he laid any groundwork? What did you do when you came in to follow up on that?

WW: Well, everybody knew it. I mean, it was in all the newspapers and speculation, and it was more or less—I mean, people pretty well knew what was coming. It was sort of general knowledge. Now, I don't think the people here as a whole had really thought very much about it. We discussed it informally, but we really hadn't taken any action until that time.

I: As far as any groundwork being laid with the board, that hadn't—

WW: Oh, we hadn't done any with the community either.

I: So there was no real preparation either by Mr. Blossom or you as far as preparing the board for this happening?

WW: As I said, Hal Douglas was on the board, and he was sort of our legal—you might say our legal representative—he was the lawyer on the board. And he kept up with it as much or more than I did. I mean, he knew as much as I did about it. And he was the one who really influenced the board.

I: Was there any threat of any kind of legal action if the board did not comply with the *Brown* decision that you are aware of? No one was threatening to intervene on behalf of the black students?

WW: No.

I: I think you may have answered this already, but let me make sure I got it correct. Were any of the school board members initially opposed to integration of the schools?

WW: No.

I: It was a pretty unanimous decision?

WW: It was unanimous.

I: Let me ask you about a couple of names here and your perception of what their role was. Mrs. Louise Bell, who was the principal at the high school at the time? What kind of input did she have or what kind of role did she play in the integration process?

WW: We really hadn't done any work with the principals other than, you know, to discuss it in principals' meeting. We talked about the possibility that this could happen, but, like I say, we really didn't have a plan.

I: Ms. Minnie Dawkins at Lincoln—would you put her in the same category?

WW: Yes, she was—this was an interesting situation because she faced the loss of her position as principal of that school if it went through, but she was strongly supportive of it even though that would happen. Of course, we had a very small [black] school, as you may recall. The black population only constituted about 3 percent of our enrollment. In fact, we only had thirteen students that were integrated the first year, and we only integrated at the high school level the first year.

I: Mr. White, was there any kind of significant organized local opposition to the integration that you were aware of?

WW: None. I would have been aware of it if there was. There wasn't.

I: Yes, I know how school administration works. You're pretty well aware if there is any opposition to anything.

WW: There were a few individuals that protested it, but, as far as I can recall, nobody ever came even to a school board meeting to protest it.

I: Now, the opposition you talk about from individuals—that came in the form of phone calls to you? Was that before or after the decision?

WW: Oh, no, it was after.

I: After the decision.

WW: After, yes. In fact, I only even remember one phone call. I only remember getting one phone call that was opposing it.

I: But no organized local opposition whatsoever.

WW: No.

I: I talked with Harry Vandergriff, who was a coach there, about the role of athletics in the process.

ww: I had breakfast with Harry this morning.

I: Did you really?

ww: Yes.

I: What's your take on what role, if any, athletics had in making this a smoother transition or not?

ww: It did. It definitely did. In fact, it made it much easier, and it also was the biggest problem that we had. I don't know how much of this you already know, but we had one student—we had been sending one student to Hot Springs because he wanted to play football, and they didn't have football at Lincoln High in Fort Smith. So we allowed him to go down there and paid his expenses.

I: This is the one called Bull.

ww: Yes, Bull Hayes. And so he came out and made starting fullback on the football team. And they—well, half the schools on our schedule canceled their games with us because of that. The board was under tremendous pressure to hold him out of games, especially when we went to another school to play. And the superintendents were afraid that there would be big trouble if a black player went out on the field, on their field.

I: When you say "under pressure," under pressure from other superintendents?

ww: Yes, yes. And, in fact, I got called some of the worse names I ever had in my life—the only time in my life—from other superintendents, one in particular. But, first of all, the football team voted to inform the school board that they didn't want to play unless he could play, and then the student council voted to support the football team, and they sent representatives to a school board meeting and asked the school board not to force the team to play against a team that wouldn't allow him to play. And the school board had been wavering a little bit because of all the pressure that was being put on, and they didn't want to create the problem at the other schools, and they were wavering a little bit as to whether or not we should go along with that. But as soon as those students came before the board and told them how they felt about it, and they felt that strongly, immediately the school board said, well, we have to back our students. And so they voted to go ahead and play him, and if the other teams didn't like it, they could cancel the game. And about half of them did.

And then the other problem that we had was that when they went to play a team—when they went away from home, they usually had a meal at a restaurant, and there was only one place that we went that we could find a restaurant that would allow him in the restaurant. And the players, again, said they wouldn't eat in a restaurant unless he could. And so the lunchroom prepared sack lunches for them to take with them, and they ate on the school bus.

i: Considering the fact that Fayetteville was so prompt to integrate this high school, what was the reason that it took so long to complete the process with the Lincoln School? I have here 1965, Lincoln Elementary School, before that process of total one-through-twelve integration was completed.

ww: '65?

i: That's what I have here in my notes—that the elementary school wasn't integrated until '65.

ww: I don't think that's right—maybe it is. Hmm. Well, did we integrate the junior high the next year? In '55?

i: It says here—the "League of Women Voters recommended that the children of the Lincoln School, the segregated Negro elementary school, should be integrated by the fall of '64. Board president Henry Shreve explained it was necessary to delay the action until '65 because of 'many problems associated with the closing of Lincoln, including relocation of black teachers.'"

ww: I didn't remember it was that long, but I guess that must be right. We worked very closely with the leaders in the black community. And, as I recall, I guess, maybe, there was a reluctance at that time—they were mainly interested in the high school, more than anything else. Thinking back now, I'm trying to remember, but it seems to me like they weren't ready to give up their school right away. And, of course, we did have three teachers over there, including Ms. Dawkins who was one of them. But I think it probably had more to do with the readiness of the black community than anything else.

Also, another problem was, where they lived it was hard to divide them so that they wouldn't all go to one school. And it was located in such a way that, as I recall, you either sent them to Washington School, which was mostly upper class and upper middle class, I mean, economically speaking, or down to Jefferson, which was a very low income area. It wasn't really the best situation to put them in either one of those situations, if you know what I mean. More likely there wouldn't have been any problems as far as whites were concerned in putting them in Washington School, but it might have been a little problem for those children, and it took us a while for this to all work itself out and for everybody to be fully supportive, especially the black parents. They were supportive in every way, and we wanted to work with them, and we did work with them.

I: Do you recall an organization called the Fayetteville Community Relations Council or Association and what role, if any, it had in the process? And also, let me ask you at the same time, about the League of Women Voters, either of those organizations.

WW: League of Women Voters was a very, very influential group. It was, more or less, the feminine leadership in the city. The other one I recall as being a—I don't want to call them a left-wing organization—but a more, a pretty much liberal organization that was, I guess you'd say, maybe out in front of the mainstream population.

I: How significant was the role of the Community Relations Council, in your opinion?

WW: Not significant. It was real small—I can only recall one or two people associated with that. We had a couple, in particular, maybe two or three, that were, what do I want to say, really liberal on practically all issues of city government. They were what I would call a minority group that was quite vocal but didn't carry the kind of political clout that you would have from a group like Association of University Women or the League of Women Voters, either one.

I: Dr. White, what position did a lady named Mrs. Pearlie Williams, who was Ms. Dawkins' successor as principal of Lincoln, take regarding the closing of Lincoln School? Do you recall anything about that, Pearlie Williams, that name?

WW: No. Yes, I recall the name, but I think she left before I came. I believe Ms. Dawkins was the principal when I came here. If not, my memory is failing me.

I: Pearlie Williams came after Ms. Dawkins.

WW: No, no. It must have been before. I think Ms. Dawkins stayed until—in fact, it might have been when she left that we totally integrated the elementary school. That may be the case.

I: Let me go back to something you said just a minute ago in regard to the black residents of Fayetteville. Was it your impression that all the black residents of Fayetteville favored integration and elimination of Lincoln School or not?

WW: If there were any that opposed it, I never did know. The leadership was strongly supportive of it. I remember the Hoover family particularly. Teresa Hoover, who I think just retired, was one of the top officials of the Methodist Church in the United States, and she was from that family. And she was very supportive and her family—they were pretty much the leaders of the community.

I guess the only problem—I remember an incident where I had a delegation of black students after we—sometime, not too long after we integrated—I think it might have been all of the black students—came to my office one afternoon after school, and they were complaining about the school lunches.

I: This was in the first year of integration?

ww: Yeah, yeah. And I said that was the best school lunch room I have ever, ever seen anywhere. It served the best meals. It was just like a commercial establishment. And so I asked them, I said, this is the first time I've ever had a complaint on the lunches at Fayetteville High School. I said, "What is it you don't like?" And they said, "Well, they don't serve soul food." And I said, "Well, you know, I grew up in the South and I've heard this expression about soul food." I said, "Tell me, what do you mean? What is soul food?" And they said, "Well, it's corn bread and turnip greens and black-eyed peas." I said, "Good grief, I grew up on it. I just didn't know I was eating soul food." I said, "I'll see what I can do about it." So I went over and talked to Ms. Brooks, Frances Brooks, the lunchroom director, and she started putting out those things on the line for students to select, and I never heard another complaint.

I: That's interesting. The first year, then, was rather smooth?

ww: Oh, yes, it was very smooth. As far as students were concerned, I never knew of any unpleasant incidents. There might have been, but they never got to me if they did.

I: Do you recall, Dr. White, any negative reaction to sending black children to these previously all-white Washington and Jefferson Elementary Schools?

ww: No, I don't, no, I don't recall. Of course, we worked very closely with the PTAs. They knew everything we were going to do after that first year when the school board suddenly decided to do it, but then, from then on, we kept them very informed. I recall no problems. The biggest problem we had was that the children in the black school were so far behind the other children that they had problems in that respect. And that was mostly because of the low economic situation they were in.

I: When you came from Siloam Springs—in 1953, did you say?

ww: Yes.

I: Did you foresee this kind of thing—that this was coming? Did you foresee this as being something that this community and this school system was going to have to deal with?

ww: Oh, sure.

I: So you weren't coming in unaware that this was a possibility this was going to occur?

ww: No. I knew it was coming. We all suspected it was coming. And, in fact, the University already had black students at the University in the law school. So that sort of broke the ice. And people, I think, here, in Fayetteville, because of that, were more aware of it than most places who never gave it a thought. Down in the South, they'd say, "Well, it doesn't matter what they say, we're not going to do anything about it." But here, I think, most people knew eventually it was going to come, although I remember one lady that after we'd been integrated for a while, I saw her at church, and she said, "You know what they're trying to do now?" I said, "What?" She said, "They're even trying to integrate the churches." [Laughs.] This lady was one who didn't—she didn't fight it, but she felt like, she felt like they were better off in their own school, particularly elementary children, and she did a lot of work over in that community helping people and so on. But she felt like they were doing them [blacks] a disservice to pull them out of their community and their school. But also, she was sort of the old school that, you know, you be good to them, but keep them in their place.

I: Dr. White, when you were considering taking the job, I assume you talked to Virgil Blossom before taking the job . . .

ww: Oh, yes.

I: In the course of those conversations, did he indicate to you what course he believed this thing might take in Fayetteville? Were you reassured?

ww: That's too far back. I don't really know. I'm sure we talked about it, and, of course, he knew it was going to come in Little Rock, too, but nobody knew the ramifications of it. I was just going to say that, that people think about Orval Faubus and the action he took in Little Rock, but never one time did I ever get any kind of communication or word from him in opposition to what we did. He was never involved at all.

I: No, no, nothing.

ww: No, because he was not a segregationist. He was a politician. And it was not politically expedient for him to get involved up here because it went well. In Little Rock, it was a big political issue, so he got involved.

I: So you never heard anything from him to the extent, "Don't do it." You never heard anything from him to the extent you were doing a good job. No input whatsoever from any kind of state agency or official.

ww: Well, you know, I was in contact with people in the State Department of Education, and I think they were pleased that it went as well as it did here.

I: So the State Department of Education looked favorably upon it, but not some of the superintendents.

ww: Right, because their jobs were on the line. You know, if your [a school superintendent's] school board is 100 percent opposed to it, how can you [not] be opposed to it if you want to keep your job?

I: How long did it take you to overcome hostility among some of them after this had happened? Is that something that lingered or something that was pretty quickly forgotten?

ww: Most of them didn't hold it against me personally, really. No, I got along well with other superintendents. There were probably a few that didn't like me because of it, but, no, I never had any problems. I was very active in the state association.

I: Looking back on this whole incident, this whole process, is there anything that stands out in your mind that I haven't discussed or we haven't discussed this morning? Anything, when you think back on this, that you'd like to relate?

ww: No, I can't think of anything. It went very smoothly, and I don't know how we could have done it any better. I think a lot of school districts made a mistake by not taking action right away, before opposition was organized against it. I mean, right at that point, most people said, "Well, it's the law; we have to do it however we're going to get it done." And what they needed was leadership from school boards, more so than superintendents. Superintendents could try to influence their board, but it really has to be the school board in a situation like that; it really needed to be the school board who were local residents, you know, who would take the responsibility for selling it to the public. And most places that didn't happen.

I: Was that the decisive factor here, do you think?

ww: Oh, without a doubt, without a doubt, because the most— see, we had a really unusual school board. And when I tell people that I was with a school board for sixteen years where we never had a split vote, they won't believe it.

I: I was a junior high principal. It's hard for me to understand in this day and age, too.

ww: Well, there was a reason for it. One was we had absolutely fantastic school board members. Secondly was that if I saw a problem developing, if somebody objected to something, we didn't just have a three-two vote. I'd back off from it, and then I would say, hey, let me get with you and talk about this. And so I'd get with board members individually, and either I would shift my position enough to make it acceptable, or maybe, in some cases, I'd just back off from it, so it wouldn't be an issue that would divide the board. And so we did things by consensus, and I had the kind of people you could do that with.

We had another situation that I've never seen anywhere else, and many, many people don't believe in it because they say it's not democratic, and, in a way, it's not. But when a board member was going off the school board, they would discuss in a board meeting who would be the best replacement for this person. And then, the chairman of the school board and I would go to that person and ask them if they would serve on the board. And only one person ever refused in sixteen years. And that was a lady. We'd never had a lady on the board, and she said, "I think you're just asking me because you want a token woman on the board, and I don't want to take it that way." And she's the only one.

OK, then, after they would agree, I would make up a petition, two copies of a petition, and I'd take it down to the two banks, and they would get their customers to sign the petition, and nobody would run against them. At that time, I don't know whether they've changed it or not, but at that time, you only had to have twenty signatures, twenty qualified voters to sign a petition to get on the ballot. We had, for sixteen years, from one to three board members every year that were up for reelection, and we were changing all the time. But in that sixteen years, we only had three people that ever ran against the person that the school board nominated, and they didn't get very many votes. But we had people like Henry Shreve, the vice-president of Campbell Soup Company, was chairman when I left here, [and] had been for several years. Like I said, Hal Douglas was the treasurer of the board for ten years or so. Then we had George Tharel, who was the manager of Penney's. We had a doctor.

We had a lawyer. Some of them were young; some of them were middle aged. But they were people that were respected in the community, and people generally, you know, most people knew who they were and had confidence in them. And so it just went amazingly well. The vice-president of the university, Charles Oxford, was also on the board. So when you had people like that, you had the cream of the crop. I was spoiled, then, when I went to Florida.

I: Not that way any more, I suppose, is it?

WW: It's not that way at all. No, it's not that way, but they developed a good school system and had fantastic support. I've never seen such support for a school system as they had here. Of course, we worked at it, and we got citizens involved. And when we needed a tax increase, when we knew we needed a big tax increase—early on after I came, we went to the University and Dr. Roy Allen's graduate students in school administration came in and worked with a citizens committee for six months to get the documentation and everything that we needed. Then we had a big citizens' meeting and they voted unanimously to support a ten mill increase, from thirty to forty mills. It took a lot of work, but we always had good support.

Thinking back to—I don't know, I really, I can't think of any other significant developments that took place as far as integration was concerned. It was—I got a lot of hate mail, but it wasn't local. It was all from south Arkansas and not from school people, but I remember I got one letter that said, "You ought to be hanging from the highest limb." Signed "Georgia White Man." But I got letters from all over the world. All of the foreign letters I remember getting were commending us for the action we took.

I: How did it break down, favorable to unfavorable, as far as your correspondence, would you say?

WW: Almost all favorable. Very few negatives.

CLARK C. McCLINTON

*Clark C. McClinton, born near Fayetteville, is a prominent business-
man and civic leader in Fayetteville. As a member of the Fayetteville
school board, he seconded the motion by Hal Douglas to begin the
integration of the city's schools in the fall of 1954.*

INTERVIEWER: I see here in the minutes of the meeting of the
school board that you seconded the motion to integrate the schools.

CLARK McCLINTON: I didn't remember that.

I: Do you remember the board meeting?

CM: Yes, I remember the meeting and deciding to do it and we
were glad to do so. We didn't think it was right for those [black]
high school kids to have to go to Fort Smith or Hot Springs to go to
school. And besides we [the school board] had to pay their expenses
down there. It was money saving to us and it was just the correct
thing to do.

I: So, you had to pay for some place for them to stay during the
week?

CM: We paid for them. Generally, they probably went where they
had some relatives or knew some people. Now, I don't remember
the details of that. But, I do know that we paid their expenses for
them to be away from home because we didn't have a school for
them. It wasn't right.

I: Did you talk about keeping the decision out of the press in the
meeting?

CM: Not at this meeting. At this meeting we just made the decision about what we were going to do. I don't remember the details.
But I am sure that in time we decided that we didn't want any hulla-
baloo about it, or the press interviewing these kids, trying to make
an issue out of it. Because, after all, it was the first school that integrated in the South and we just didn't want anything to be disrup-

tive. I don't know when those decisions were made, but I would say pretty soon after that.

I: I thought it was interesting that the decision about the press was made at all.

CM: We felt sure the press would be interested in the first Southern school to integrate, and we did not want a big issue over it in the press. We decided that news reporters would be allowed on the school grounds. It turned out that there was an AP reporter present, and we did not allow him to go into the school and disrupt the classes and interview the students.

I: Do you remember anything about the decision about the blacks being able to play on the athletic teams?

CM: That is on that next page there [of the minutes of meetings]. It so happens that when that decision was made I wasn't at that meeting. But I knew about it, and I knew what they were going to do. And I think that they had a meeting at the school with the football players. And they decided that the kids were there, and they had a right to be there and that if those other schools wouldn't play us then they just wouldn't play us. I think that there were three schools that wouldn't play us that year. I don't know how much time went by before they did play us. It didn't last very long.

I: Tell me about the town at the time. How segregated was the town of Fayetteville?

CM: Well, I know that a black man couldn't get a haircut in the barbershop. I don't think that the black people could stay in the hotels. I had been in and around Fayetteville all my life, and there weren't that many black people in Fayetteville. Integration, to me, was not a big issue. I do know that when we integrated the grade schools a few years later, we wanted to be sure that the black kids were divided between Jefferson School and Washington School, and it made several of the white parents mad because we divided them. They thought that they would all go to Jefferson. We deliberately divided the town so that about half would go to one and half to the other. There were some people that had a very strong feeling about integration. They were just opposed to integration. Very opposed. They were not in the majority. Some of the school board members had telephone calls from friends when we integrated the grade schools and they were very unhappy. I did not receive any calls.

I: With the grade school, but nothing with the high school?

CM: Well, what was it, six of them? That wasn't very many. But to these people in their own minds, they just didn't want their little elementary school kids to be around little black kids and that's all there was to it—I had no calls from any people who were opposed to it, but some of the former board members were glad that they had gotten off the board before integration. . . .

I: How long did you stay on?

CM: Ten years.

I: Were your kids in school?

CM: David was in high school. I think John Lewis was in the first class that the black kids had gone to all three years of the school, and David was a year older than him. He was in school when these kids entered.

I: Did he [David McClinton] ever say anything to you about it?

CM: No, he never mentioned it. We tried to keep it from being an issue. When we integrated the elementary school, I remember going down to the Lincoln School to talk to the parents. And we said it is going to depend a lot on you parents about how successful this is going to be. . . . There was a general meeting of the black people. Many of the black parents were not in favor of integrating the elementary grades. They felt that the Lincoln School was their school and it was a center of interest for them.

I: Mrs. Louise Bell [principal of Fayetteville High School] said that Minnie Dawkins, the principal of Lincoln School, did a lot to prepare the parents and the students for the integration.

CM: She was a very fine lady and did a good job. . . . You have to remember that there weren't very many black people in Fayetteville. And it wasn't a big issue. It wasn't like in the areas where it was 50 percent black, or 60 percent black. And the people in northwest Arkansas as a whole were not that concerned about it—there was very little prejudice that I can remember. A few people were very strongly opposed to integration . . . I don't remember the exact circumstances, but there was a black man in town and he said that he couldn't go anywhere to get a haircut. Now that is bad when you can't go anywhere to get a haircut. . . . I know that they could not go into a restaurant to eat.

I: Did that sort of segregation stop soon after the Supreme Court decision?

CM: It never was a big issue here because there weren't many black people. That came about probably in the 1960s more than at that time. There were people that at first, when they saw a black person in a restaurant, would leave, but there wasn't anything else they could do about it. My dad was from Alabama, and he had all of the prejudices of a Southerner to integration. A black person couldn't call a white person by their first name, it was Mr. so-and-so and Miss so-and-so, and Southerners felt very strongly about it.

I: Did you grow up here?

CM: Yes, I was born here and my first memories are of a farm that my grandfather Newkirk bought north of Springdale in 1885. . . . You have to remember that there weren't that many black people in Fayetteville. My father told me there was a sign on the outskirts of Rogers that stated, "Black man, don't let the sun set on you here." . . . To my knowledge, no black person lived in Springdale until the 1980s.

Bentonville and Fayetteville and Cane Hill, Arkansas, are the oldest towns in these two counties, and there were black slaves in those communities prior to the Civil War; these black people gradually moved out of Cane Hill and Bentonville into Fayetteville. The hollow that U.S. Highway 62 follows up the Lincoln Mountain about two miles east of Lincoln, Arkansas, is called "Bud Kidd Hollow." Also there is a lake about one mile north from there named "Bud Kidd Lake." Bud Kidd was a black man who lived in that hollow at the turn of the century.

There just weren't that many black people in this area. So, there wasn't the prejudice like there was built in in other areas where there were bigger populations. . . .

That's what shocked people in the North. They just thought that prejudice was a problem in the South, but they had just as many problems or more in the North when they integrated schools as we did in the South. The Southern people as a whole, so I've been told, like individual black people, but not the race as a whole. But they have black friends. In the North, it just was not that a way. They probably had more trouble integrating in the North. . . .

The reason that the NAACP chose Little Rock, this is just me talking now, is that Arkansas was farther along with their racial relations than any other southern state, and so they chose Little Rock. But you know that those inhibitions against blacks were just as strong in the Little Rock area as they were in any other area. But as a whole Arkansas had better racial relations than any other southern state. . . . I believe that is the reason that Little Rock was chosen as the big city to integrate. . . .

I: Did blacks attend the University?

CM: Not many at this time. The first black student to attend the University was a law student. And they let him enter, but they had him sit in a place with a rail around it. . . . It so happened that the white students didn't think that was right so they took that rail down. Somebody told me this who was either a professor or a student at the University at the time. I don't remember when that happened, but I think it was in the late forties [1948].

To me, integration was just the right thing to do. But you know that there were some die-hards everywhere, and they didn't like the idea of black students going to a white school.

I: Where did you say they sent the black high school students?

CM: They were either going to Fort Smith or Hot Springs, either place that they wanted to go because they both had black schools, black high schools. And whichever place they preferred going, that is my memory about it. But we had to pay their expenses, and most of them would go where they had relatives or where they had friends.

I: It sounds like it [integration] all went so smoothly.

CM: It did. A lot of it is just the fact that we just didn't have a large black population here. And we had people that felt that it just wasn't right for those kids to have to go away. Whenever it came up, to me and to those of us on that [school] board, there just wasn't anything else to do but to integrate the schools. And the reason we didn't integrate any further was that we had a school for them. . . .

We never thought of it as being a historic thing. In fact, we didn't know at the time that we were the first to do it. I didn't realize it. It was just the natural thing for us to do. I will say it again. There were two reasons—it wasn't right to send those kids away from home and make them stay away from home, and it was costing the school district money that could be better utilized in education rather than room and board and expenses. I'm glad we did. It was the time to do it. I'm sure that if there hadn't been a [state] law against it we would have already integrated earlier, but by the law we could not. . . .

I remember getting a letter after we integrated the high school. I don't know whether from a man or woman, from somewhere in Mississippi, that said they couldn't believe that we had integrated and that they hoped that my daughter had to marry a black man, and the school board ought to be hung.

WILLIAM C. MORTON JR.

William C. Morton Jr., a native of Fayetteville, was a life insurance agent during his tenure as a member of the Fayetteville school board. He was a member of the board in 1954 when the decision was made to desegregate the city's schools.

WILLIAM C. MORTON JR.: My memory's not quite that sharp. I remember a whole lot about that thing, but I don't remember that much about dates. You might like to have a copy of the minutes.

INTERVIEWER: All right.

WCM: Let me just cover these minutes, and then you can start any place you want to, Tom, but on May 21, 1954, the board met at the old Washington Hotel. We met there at a private dining room. We met there for lunch frequently. All members were present. We learned at that meeting about the Supreme Court decision. And we made the motion right then that we were going to abide by that thing, and we'd just as well do it the following September. So people had from May 21 until September to get ready. There were no outcries, no demonstrations, none of that kind of stuff. But what we hadn't thought about was what we would do if one of the black students, you know, went out for football or basketball or some other contact sport and made the team. That didn't occur until a year from the following September.

But in September of 1955, fall 1955 football season, there were two or three black boys that went out for football. Harry Vandergriff was the coach then. . . . And they stuck it out, and they made the team, albeit the third team, something like that. And so, Wayne White was superintendent of schools then, and Wayne got a call or a letter from Fort Smith. We were the first district to integrate, and a lot of the other districts didn't like that because we did it so quick. But we had a reason for doing it. And so none of the rest of them had integrated, so, of course, there were no blacks on any of their football teams. And the Fort Smith superintendent got hold of Wayne White and said, you know, we want to play you, but we'd like for you to leave your black boys at home when you play Fort Smith.

So the students—first, I think, the football team, when they heard about that, they objected to it badly because those boys had stuck it out, and there were only three of them. And you see what happened there, when Superintendent White informed the board that he had been notified by Fort Smith that they couldn't compete with integrated schools—even if they had to forfeit. We said, look, let's just agree to cancel that game, and we just felt that was the right thing to do. We'd already made up our mind, and that was the end of that—I'll tell you the rest of that story. We had always had a black grade school called Lincoln School. It was the first eight grades. And we never had a black high school, so we were transporting our black students to Fort Smith when they got through the eighth grade to go to high school down there, and then later, just before I went on the board, we transported them to both Fort Smith and to Hot Springs.

I: I read that somewhere, but how did that work?

WCM: I'm not really sure about that. I wasn't on the board then, and I don't know anybody that would know about that.... Probably they just sent them down there and had some place for them to stay, but—then when we went to the junior high deal, we just still kept that black grade school with eight grades in it and only had about two teachers down there, but they were outstanding black teachers. And so we had received a letter from the Fort Smith school district and from Hot Springs both prior to the time that this Supreme Court decision was made, that they would not be able to take our black students because of their overcrowded condition beginning in September of 1955. So we didn't know what we were going to do with them because we just didn't know.

So when the Supreme Court decision came out, we made our decision that we would integrate. And if you will read this [school board minutes] carefully, you will note that it says—the motion is that "Negro pupils living in the Fayetteville School District be admitted to Fayetteville Senior High School in September, 1954." That meant we started integrating at the high school level. We didn't integrate all the way through because the Lincoln School was situated in the very middle of the black residential section. And because of those fine teachers, we just felt like it was in their best interest to have that grade school continue and have those little kids, you know, going to school down there where they were close to home, and they would be better prepared when it came time for junior high. So we integrated the senior high school first, then junior high, and then some years later we integrated the grade schools. . . .

I: Seems like I read something to the effect it was around 1965. Does that sound right? When the Lincoln School went out of operation.

WCM: I just don't remember, but I know it stayed in operation for quite a few years after we integrated the high school.

I: Was there ever any discussion of alternative plans other than integration of the high school?

WCM: No. No. This date right here, on May twenty-first, we made that decision, and there were never any other considerations.

I: Did the members of the board at that time anticipate that this would be an unpopular decision in the community? I guess what I'm wanting to know is, it's my understanding that there was some ground—had been some groundwork laid for this before this took place in the community in terms of the churches and the schools, perhaps, and maybe even involving the University. To what extent were they involved, if at all?

WCM: I don't believe they were involved at all. I think we knew we were going to have to do something with the senior high students, but there wasn't anything to discuss about it because we had not yet tried to make a decision on it. You've got to remember in 1953 and '54, schools were crowded, and school property was all run down because it hadn't been replaced or added to during World War II, and, see, that was only eight years after the end of World War II. And it takes time to get a replacement program cranked up and get your millage voted and bond issues and all those things. So, we were terribly crowded, just like Fort Smith and just like Hot Springs.

So, so far as I know, there was no work done on that before that decision was made. I went on the school board in about 1953. I'd been on it about a year when this occurred. And maybe it was a little less than a year. Hal Douglas and I went on at the same time. And a year later, two other fellows went off and two came on. But— it went smoothly. We didn't have any problems. We didn't anticipate any problems. We wouldn't have been able to do anything if there had been some problems so far as that decision was concerned, because we had no place to put them.

I: Well, why do you think the community seemed to accept this move here whereas in other places, not only in Arkansas but throughout the South, there was a great deal of opposition to this kind of program? I guess what I'm referring to—was there some basis for good racial relations in Fayetteville that had been established prior to this time? Or relationships between the races?

WCM: Yes. There was, there was never any bad relation between the races. We had about the same number of blacks in Fayetteville then that we had fifty years ago as I recall it, about four hundred, and so it was a very small black population, percentage-wise, compared with the black population in most of the rest of the state. We didn't anticipate any problems, and, you know, the school board had—the schools had such good relations with the community. We've never suffered a bond issue defeat. We've never suffered a millage defeat, and just had real good relations with the community. And we felt like they would accept the decision, particularly when they understood it. And they did. The only time we had any concerns about things were when this came up, and we had to take a stand on being integrated throughout the whole system. You know, debate, basketball, football, study hall, everything. And we just never varied from that at all. We really didn't have any problem.

There were—on the day that the fall semester started in 1954— we were told that there were photographers and reporters that came to Fayetteville from all of the major surrounding newspapers. They came from, you know, Kansas City and Little Rock, Tulsa and Oklahoma City. They came from all around, I don't know all of the ones. Some may have come from a lot farther than that, expecting some kind of incident, and there were just simply no pictures taken. Nothing happened. The black kids showed up for school, and they went to class, and there was never—there wasn't a problem.

I: There's an article in the *Christian Century* about the fact that there was an AP photographer who had shot some photographs, but because there was no problem, they canceled plans to have any more people come down. So apparently there was anticipation that there might be a problem, but it just didn't happen here.

WCM: That's right. They were expecting one.

I: What about the interim period before the decision in May? There are a couple of questions I want to ask you about that. Is this something that you or other members of the board had seen coming? Did the *Brown* decision catch you off guard in terms of when it came or is it something that you had anticipated for some time would happen, possibly might happen while you were on the board?

WCM: We never dwelled on that. There was never any discussion about it. I'd been on the board less than a year when that decision was made. And as soon as we got it, we acted; so there was no hesitancy, and there was no real preparation for it.

I: So it wasn't a case of the decision comes out and board members, perhaps, get together and talk about the need for unanimity; it was just something you hadn't discussed really with them until the board meeting, what, four or five days later?

WCM: Yes. On May twenty-first. That's the first board meeting where we had any discussion.

I: Do you recall the discussion leading up to the motion being made? What was said?

WCM: Yes, I remember in essence what was said. Hal Douglas— Hal was [U.S. Senator J. William] Fulbright's brother-in-law, fine man, and Hal married Helen Fulbright, Bill's younger sister, and, you know, at that meeting, Hal said, "Well, boys, the Supreme Court decision came down, and here's what it says." Hal was a lawyer. And so, it was the feeling of all of us that that answered the problem of what we were going to do about it in the fall of 1955. And we talked about it briefly, and someone said, "Well, why should we wait until the fall of '55? Those people in Fort Smith and in Hot Springs need that space now. Why don't we just do it now and get it done?" And that's exactly what we did. That thing wasn't discussed more than that—that meeting didn't last any longer than the normal meetings.

I: So there was no long, drawn-out debate over this issue.

WCM: No, no arguments about it, no nothing. Nobody felt any differently than anybody else. It was something that we just had to do.

I: In the interim between the decision in May and the start of school in September, what kind of input did you get from the community in the anticipation of the starting of school.

WCM: Very little. Very little. We decided that, right or wrong, when we put those students into the system in the high school it wouldn't make any difference. But in the grade schools, we would have to spread them evenly throughout all the grade schools. And so those are just some basic decisions that were made for the time when we would grow into the fully integrated system in the grade schools and in the junior high. This only affected the senior high at that time.

I: That's ten, eleven, and twelve.

WCM: Right. So then, it was the seven, eight, nine that would be next, but we just didn't know exactly when that would be because— I don't remember what we did with those eighth-grade students.

I: Seventy-six were sophomores, I think it said, in that year.

WCM: I believe that eighth-grade students stayed. What did we do with the ninth grade, I don't remember. I don't know what we did with the ninth-grade kids. Maybe kept them in Lincoln School.

I: I guess I want to get back to the question of what it was about the situation in Fayetteville that was different from that throughout much of the rest of the South where we see massive resistance to the policy of integration of schools.

WCM: It was probably mostly numbers. Mostly numbers. And, you know, you have to attribute some of that to those teachers. . . .

I: Had the University been integrated prior to this? Were black students in the university system?

WCM: Yes, yes.

I: Was that, did that have any effect or not, do you think, on the situation in the public school?

WCM: If it did, I'm not aware of it. I wasn't aware of it at the time. Of course, it did not have a bad effect, I know that. There was just never any—never a problem on the University campus.

I: Were you surprised at all that there weren't any problems when school began?

WCM: Little bit, yes. Little bit. But, you know, we had a good teaching staff and good, just good people in the school system. And I tell you, the University did have an outstanding effect on the Fayetteville system, and that's because—you know, you had to pay such low salaries then. Just terrible, the salaries that we paid because we couldn't do anything different. But we were always blessed in the Fayetteville district with teachers who were wives of graduate students, wives of young faculty members, wives of any faculty members, that were here because their husbands were either graduate students or professors at the University—well qualified, extremely well qualified—that taught in the Fayetteville system that we could not have attracted on salary alone. So that influence was present for all purposes.

I: You mentioned numbers. If it had been sixty black students instead of six, do you think the response might have been substantially different?

WCM: Probably. If it had been six hundred, you know, it would have been different. I imagine just the sheer weight of numbers was the difference in here and some of the southern districts. Little Rock, you know, obviously had all kinds of things involved in that Little Rock problem. And we just didn't have those outside influences involved here. They were pretty well left alone to go ahead about the business of going to school.

I: You alluded to this a minute ago, but it seems that a lot of the problems in Little Rock and other places came from outside influences who were determined to disrupt the integration, like segregationist organizations or individuals. Did you get any kind of outside pressure here as a school board member? Did faculty or administrators get that, to your knowledge?

WCM: Not to my knowledge. I received none. There were some people in town who were friends of everybody on that board that were bitterly opposed to it and didn't like it. But they didn't do anything about it. I knew every one of them. We had a group of people around town that would buy season tickets [for football] to the high school games. Not season tickets; they'd buy books of tickets. However many they were asked to buy. And Harry [Vandergriff, football coach] ran into one of them that wouldn't buy any tickets because of integration. But you had things like that that took place that didn't make any headlines, and nobody knew anything about it. So, but those were isolated cases, Tom. They just were not—didn't involve groups of people, you know.

When you get groups of people, then you've got trouble. You've got one group of people, then you've got another group of people, and then you've got people from the outside trying to influence it. I'm told that took place in Little Rock. That was the worst scene, I guess, that we had in the state, Little Rock. And both sides thought they were right. But, you know, I knew Virgil Blossom very well, the superintendent of schools down there when that happened. And Blossom was the high school football coach when I was in high school here, and he's the guy that came to see me about serving on the school board. And he was the superintendent of schools then, here, and a superb superintendent. After he went to Little Rock, that thing blew up. I don't mean that Blossom caused it; he didn't.

But he was there when it happened. And we'd see him up here during football season. His daughter was still going to the University. And all the board members used to see Virgil, you know, and needle him about the mess "he caused" down there and that kind of stuff. Blossom was the one that everybody (his friends) needled. But, you know, he used to tell us, "Boys, this is a different story down there." He said, "Those folks aren't going to let that happen." So, I know it was a lot different, just from hearsay.

I: What made the situation in Fayetteville different, do you think, from surrounding Arkansas communities like Rogers, Fort Smith, Springdale?

WCM: Springdale didn't have any blacks. Rogers had probably none. Bentonville had very, very few. So they had no problem at all. Fort Smith, you know, then you're into the numbers. And where we had sixty or whatever it was—where we had four hundred population in Fayetteville, they might have had fifteen thousand or twenty thousand. That's a big difference.

I: Now, you were in what business at the time that you decided to run for the school board in '54.

WCM: I was in the life insurance business.

I: Did you have any inkling at all at the time that this might develop during your term?

WCM: No. Never gave it a thought.

I: Would that have influenced your decision if you had known this kind of momentous decision might be coming?

WCM: No, it wouldn't have influenced me. You don't let things like that influence you when Virgil Blossom comes to see you to run for school board. It just seemed like the right thing to do, you know. So, no, I wouldn't have given that any thought.

I: So as far as being affected personally or in a business sense by the decision, you couldn't tell any difference in your personal relationships in your business?

WCM: None at all. None at all. I don't know anybody on the board that felt any pressures from a business standpoint.

I: How important, Mr. Morton, was the economic consideration in the decision to integrate? Would that factor into it, the fact that Fayetteville had been paying quite a bit, I assume, to bus these children somewhere else, and now those facilities were not available? Did that figure into the decision at all?

WCM: We didn't try to equate it, what we were spending then to what we would be spending fully integrated. There wasn't any need to do that. Because there was no choice. You know, when it's the law of the land, that eliminates a lot of research. No, I wouldn't say that entered into it at all.

I: When the court ruled later that this should be accomplished "with all deliberate speed," that certainly was interpreted differently in a lot of places than it was in Fayetteville with the promptness with which you acted on it. Did you feel under any restraints of time as far as the integration of the remainder of the system, as far as what plans you would make to integrate the remainder of the system—junior high, elementary?

WCM: Did we feel any pressures on that?

I: Or what kind of time frame did you begin to look at in terms of doing that?

WCM: Well, we didn't really know. Our concerns were what was the best thing for those [black] students because for generations they had all gone to that school [Lincoln School] down there, and it was right next door to a lot of their houses, and it was a part of their community. And, you know, to suddenly close that thing down and put those students into classrooms of, let's say, we had an average of thirty-five in a classroom at that time—it might have been a little better than that, maybe thirty best, you might have two or three black children in a classroom with thirty whites as opposed to being in a black school down there where all the grades were black. And we just didn't know. We were just—we were, we felt pretty cautious about it. But we knew we had to go ahead and get it done based on some kind of plan. But that was the main thing that we always thought about. You know, how is this going to impact on those kids. I thought the board really took the noble position on that.

I: In addition to yourself and the other members of the board, were there any other individuals who you would say were instrumental in making this smooth transition that went off basically without any incidents at all, people either in the community or in the schools that you could cite as being particularly important to the orderly transition?

WCM: Well, the people who were critical of it were absolutely in the minority. It was—the whole community was responsible for it going as smoothly as it did. Just didn't have any problems. Now, when those kids first got there—we're talking about now when we got the grade schools integrated. When they first got there, they were just sort of into everything, you know. They wanted to be a part of this and a part of that. And pretty soon, that kind of changed a little bit, I am told by the administration, and that they would sort of cluster around each other, and were a little bit stand-offish, but that was just a pendulum that seemed to swing back and forth. Never were there any problems or demonstrations of any kind inside the school or outside of it—during the time I was on the board. Never.

I: You talked earlier, Mr. Morton, about meeting with some student representatives. What feeling did you get from them as to how they felt about this process or this transition that was going to be made?

WCM: Well, after the integration was made, they took the position that the school should be integrated in every respect. You couldn't integrate it for purposes of attending classes and not integrate it for purposes of being on the debate team and being on one of the athletic teams, and so on. They were exactly right. They were looking at it exactly as they should have. So I think the young people showed remarkable ability to move with the times.

I: What strikes me about the minutes of this meeting is it's so matter of fact. You're talking about two things, and one is laying the sewer line, and the other one is this integration of the school, and it's just so routine, that's very striking there.

WCM: Jack Roberts was a super guy. He'd been a scoutmaster for I don't know how many years and just an old, you know, and he'd done a lot of work and helped the school a lot, and he wanted—I don't know why he wanted to put a sewer line across Harmon field, but, you know, if you're going to let anybody do something, you know, we would have wanted to let Jack do it.

I: With regard to the athletic problems you encountered with the attempt to play teams other than Fort Smith; I think you said Russellville and Harrison. Did that continue into the next year also?

WCM: Ah, I don't know, but it didn't continue very long because they got some black boys that could run and could tackle, and then we had a hard time beating them.

I: How important was athletics, do you think, in terms of high school or college in terms of speeding along the process of integration? Do you see that as an important factor or not?

WCM: Why, I guess it is. You know, because those, a lot of those boys have good athletic ability, and the good ones are—they're bet-

ter than a lot of good white ones. They're just good. And it's given
them an opportunity to produce something, and I think that's got
to be good. There's probably a down side to it. I don't know what it is.

I: Here's a copy of the *Gazette* on May 23, 1954, announcing
Fayetteville was going to integrate. And it talks about how Sheridan
in Grant county had also voted to integrate, but then because of
community pressure, the school board had voted to rescind that
integration order.

WCM: Yes. I wonder what you would do if you were in the same
relative position as Little Rock?

I: It would be different, I suppose.

WCM: Yes. But, you know, if my telephone had rung many a night,
friends calling up and saying, Bill, what in the world are you doing
trying to sell me on the idea of undoing it. You know, you wonder,
but I don't believe our board would have changed anything.

LOUISE SHORES BELL

Louise Shores Bell, born in Malden, Missouri, has resided in the Fayetteville area since 1922. An English teacher at Fayetteville High School from 1927 to 1945, she became principal in the latter year and remained in that position until July 1, 1956. Mrs. Bell played a highly significant role in initiating and implementing desegregation of the town's school system.

INTERVIEWER: I think that it is remarkable that our school board took the initiative five days after the Supreme Court decision and then you and somebody else made it happen really smoothly.

LOUISE SHORES BELL: Well, you know it was partly just smart financing. You realize that. Preston Lackey, I can't remember—I should have written this down, but Preston Lackey was in an Oklahoma school and I guess he was a junior when he came back.

I: Yes, he was, I saw it in the yearbook.

LB: But that was a good school board. That is another thing, they don't have people on the school board now with the political or business experience that that school board had. I was saying today that I thought that one of the smartest things that [school superintendent] Virgil Blossom did was to keep it out of the paper until after it was an accomplished fact.

I: Virgil was superintendent and Wayne White came in the next summer, is that right?

LB: Virgil went the year we integrated. He missed the integration; he had set it all up, but then he went to Little Rock. And that was a horrible shock, I can tell you. Minnie Dawkins was the principal over at Lincoln school. She did so much to get the families and the children ready for this. And she and I had a lot of conferences before it happened. Really, in the fall before Virgil left.

I: What kinds of things did you do to get them ready?

LB: Well, she [Minnie Dawkins] talked about which areas the students who were coming in were the weakest in. And we talked about which courses they should take then. Then, of course, before school started, we had the parents who wanted to come and the children go all through the building to get acquainted with the building. . . . The teachers were there, and you remember the 26 Club. Ruth Boggs's 26 Club helped participate in the summer, not really an orientation, but to get acquainted so that the parents would know what it looked like where they were coming.

[To John Lewis] Do you remember that we had an organization called Sophomore Guides? Well, you didn't need them, so you don't remember them. We had this organization, and their whole purpose was to help with the orientation of sophomores when they came in. And each sophomore, if he would put up with them, had a sponsor, or a brother or sister, or whatever you want to call it, that would help him find his classes and so on.

I: And the building was new, too.

LB: Yes, that is right. And that Sophomore Guide business applied to all the white children to see the '52 class coming in.

I: Was the building open then in 1952?

LB: I guess it was finished in '52, yes.

I: It has been said that there weren't any confrontations in the hallways, between the blacks and whites.

LB: There weren't any? No there weren't. Of course, you students probably would have known it before anyone else. But I never had any white student come to the office and complain about what a black child had done, or a teacher either. I guess it was really miraculous. I think that a lot of the credit goes to Miss Dawkins.

I: And you.

LB: She instilled in them the right attitude. Not a meek subservient attitude, but a cooperative, understanding attitude.

I: And you fixed the white students up.

LB: Well, I don't know whether I did anything about it or not. But I think the attitude was very good. Mrs. [G. C.] Ellis did an awful lot with the student council, and of course, Ruth Boggs with the 26 Club. Those organizations we had in those days were really active; it was not just names and something to belong to.

I: So the students were told at the high school like the year before that next year there would be black students coming to school?

LB: No.

I: They didn't know?

LB: No, not until we called the Sophomore Guides in and the 26 Club in in the summer time. It never got out. And it never got in the paper.

I: Was that deliberate?

LB: Yes, of course, we weren't as smart then as we would be now, but we felt that the media would not help us any and that locally it might antagonize people, and it would worry people. There wasn't anything—if it was going to happen, just let it happen, and not let people worry and take sides and get crossways about it.

I: Did you ever have any parents come to you complaining about the decision?

LB: You mean the white parents? Not a single one. And there were some pretty rabid Southerners who could have. The whole thing was just really unbelievably easy. The *New York Times* called and wanted to know all about it. And I said, well, we had so many children enter school this year and so many of them were black, and so many were white, and that is all there is to it. "Oh," he said, "I want to know about what kind of incidents you had." I said there weren't any incidents. "Oh," he said, "come on."And I said there won't be any either if the media will leave us alone. And he didn't talk to me much longer.

That is important, I think, in anything. The right of information, you know. Everybody has the right to know everything. Sometimes that is disastrous for everybody to know everything before it is for-mulated and before it has had a chance to be really organized and get underway—I don't think you can overemphasize the fact that it was handled so beautifully by Virgil [Blossom] and the school board, that there was really no time for anybody to agitate any trou-ble. And after a thing is successfully accomplished, it is kind of hard to agitate. But as to individual people, I couldn't name you a single person who was antagonistic. And certainly none of the teachers. I think that—have you talked to Harry Vandergriff?

I: I did. He told me that there was one person, he didn't name names, that was a supporter of the football team. And this person stopped buying tickets when the blacks came into the school.

LB: I didn't know that. I didn't know that at all. I am glad I didn't know that person. Well, when Johnnie Burnett—there was no love lost between us—when he was chairman of the athletic commission in the state's education department he was the one who said that the other schools in the conference don't have to play you, because you have black people.

Did I tell you this? About calling all the student representatives in? We called them in; we had a meeting. We had the members of the student council, and we had the members of the 26 Club. And we had all the football boys and all the basketball boys; track was not very important then; most of them came from the other two teams anyway. And the three faculty representatives and the coaches. I read them the statement that Johnnie Burnett had made. And I said that we have to face this, they are not going to play us—it wasn't if they [blacks] played, it was if they were on the squad. And I said I believe it is up to you to decide whether you want to eliminate the black boys from the team or whether you want to make the sacrifice of not getting to play in the conference. And so far as I know, and Harry said that's the way he remembered it, there was not one dissenting vote. And they thought it would be a disgrace if they kept the black boys from playing. . .

I: Well, I was talking to Coach Vandergriff about the fact there wasn't much discrimination in the town, like the restaurants in Fayetteville served blacks. There wasn't any real segregation in the city itself. Is that what you remember?

LB: I don't imagine that they went to the restaurants. I don't ever remember seeing them in one. Probably to drive-ins. It is a wonder that the colored people have not universally developed a very mean attitude, isn't it? Resentment boiling over for all these years inside of them. And we have so few. We really don't have much to fear. If any community could be generous in their attitude, it seems to me that Fayetteville could. Well, I just don't remember making any particular effort. I really can't think of anything I did, except call that one meeting. And I think that my philosophy was that the less we meddled with it the better off we were.

I: But you ran a very highly disciplined school.

LB: Well, maybe so.

I: But you did. I don't know how you did, but you did.

LB: Well, I don't think I was mean.

I: No, you weren't.

LB: I just think that we all had a good time together. I think most students enjoyed being there.

I: Why do you think that is?

LB: Well, because that the students participated in a lot of the running of the school. And we had homerooms then, and a student stayed in the same homeroom with the same homeroom teacher for the three years he was in high school. We had it back when we had ninth graders, so it was four years. And individual homerooms developed a lot of homeroom patriotism . . . homeroom spirit. And we had a lot of things they more or less competed in. Oh, they competed in decorating their doors for, well the 26 Club was in charge of that, I can't remember what is was for, maybe it was Colors Day. And we developed Colors Day because we didn't think it was right for the basketball players not to have something like homecoming. And a lot of those things that we did, the students thought of. And then these student organizations, the president and the secretary and treasurer of each organization, along with its sponsor, took three days and went to Mount Magazine. And now they would call it a retreat, but we just said we went for a meeting. And we discussed all these things, school problems. And I think maybe the students were better informed and therefore had a better attitude toward the things that administration did do. But I strongly believed in that activities committee. They had a lot of influence and they had a lot of good ideas; they worked hard, had a lot of school spirit.

I: What was the 26 Club?

LB: 26 club was organized by Ruth Boggs [a teacher], and she had homeroom 26, and she was going to be the sponsor and then they limited their membership to 26. And their purpose was to do anything that would be helpful in any school activity. . . . Anything that the school did that they could help with, the 26 Club helped. And it was a good experience for the sponsors and the student representatives to have as intimate an association as they did when they went to these retreats. And you see if you were a member of an organization and happened to be an officer; then you got to go nearly every year. And those students, most of them were influential students. I don't know what their activity program is now. I have not been over there, I haven't meddled in any way. I am a strong believer in well-organized and well-supervised activities. The classroom has to be formal. To get to know one another you have to have some other opportunity, I think. And I just enjoyed it, that's all. It was hard for me to quit.

I: How long were you principal?

LB: I taught English for nineteen years and was principal for eleven.

FERIBA T. MCNAIR

Feriba T. McNair, a native of DeQueen, Arkansas, was a physical edu-
cation teacher at Fayetteville High School in 1954. She later served for
six terms as a member of the Fayetteville school board (1967-86).

INTERVIEWER: Do you remember how you found out about the decision to integrate the high school?

FERIBA T. McNAIR: I don't remember a meeting. I had started teaching physical education in November of 1953, around Thanksgiving, to fill a vacancy. It was the next fall that integration took place. I knew in advance that it was going to take place. Mrs. [Louise] Bell had told us that she was going to handle it with a minimum of publicity and controversy. I remember that the black students came, and I remember gathering . . . on the steps down from the front door where the media came in, and Mrs. Bell gave them just so much time to record what the students had to say and to do the interviews and then they left. I don't remember the day being interrupted at all. I think it was early in the day.

I: Was that the first day of school?

FM: I don't remember if it was the first day of school. Does anybody else?

I: As far as we can put together, there wasn't anyone there the first day of school. But apparently there were some press that did come at some point to cover it.

FM: I think that school started and later on in the week the press arrived, but the business with the press was handled very quietly. School just started as usual, and the students—including the black students—came to school and went to their regular classes. As I remember it, on Friday of that week the national press was there. Mrs. Bell allowed them a limited amount of time for interviews. The information was that there were not many eligible black students.

They had been going to Fort Smith, and just certain students were eligible according to the standards. I assume that it was academic standards. I do remember that Mr. Blossom had been involved in selecting the students, and he was very concerned that none of the girls was pregnant. If I remember right, there were five girls and one boy that year.

I: You taught what classes?

FM: Girls' physical education. I was head of the girls' physical education department, and I taught one science course. I taught five periods of physical education. Each class had from sixty to seventy-five students because all girls were required to take physical education each year. A few were excused for health reasons, and a few were excused because their religion did not allow them to wear the shorts that were required for the PE classes.

We had open campus at noon, and on the west side was a parking lot. Teachers always had to supervise the students before school, at noon, and after school. John Lewis had a car, and it would fill up with students to go somewhere to eat. All the kids liked him, including the black kids, and there were two or three of the black students who would pile in there along with the white students. I remember noticing that sometimes some of them got to ride and sometimes they didn't, but it wasn't because they were black. It seemed to me that they [the black students] felt perfectly free to join in whatever was going on. That I remember particularly.

The other thing I remember is that some of the girls in my physical education class made a very distinct point of not going into a shower where a black student had gone. As part of the points system, girls were not absolutely required to shower, but they received points for doing so, in keeping with the physical education guidelines of cooling the body down after exercise. So, that was a kind of undercurrent of discrimination going on, but I didn't pay too much attention to it. I observed that it was going on, but I didn't criticize the girls or assign them to showers or so forth. And it just kind of got to where the black girls got into a couple of the showers, and the others went into their own favorite showers.

The other thing that I remember is that I was the supervising teacher for the cheerleaders and the Pep Club. We had pep convocations at that time, and we had homerooms. Peggy Taylor was in Homeroom 209, I believe. Anyway, the homeroom she was in—this was in 1955 or 1956—won the Homecoming Pep Rally Skit. Each homeroom presented a skit, and the winner was declared by applause. Peggy had a beautiful voice and she sang, and it just brought the house down. And the students were just—anyway they won with her presentation, and everybody in the homeroom was just gathered in this bunch hugging and cheering because they won. And it was just so wholesome, I mean really it was just a receptive thing, as far as black students were concerned.

The others I remember were the two Lackey girls, Roberta and Elnora, and their brother, the three of them from one family. The girls were very pretty and were always smiling. I believe they were well received and their smiles were sincere. I remember Mary Blackburn too—tall and quiet, always cooperative and pleasant. Another of the girls was Virginia Smith. I was pleased to see this summer, when I read her daughter's wedding announcement, that her daughter had graduated from college.

And the other thing: has anyone told you about the school year that no one would play us? Have they told you about the committee that the board set up?

I: Coach Vandergriff said that certain teams would not play us if we brought our black players. There was a meeting to ask the team whether they wanted to let the black kids play and not get to play those teams, or not to let the black kids play. And that it was a unanimous vote for not playing those teams.

FM: I think that the whole thing was well done because the board set up a committee of students and teachers. There may have been parents on it. I don't remember who all was on it, but I was on it. We heard all of the pros and cons, and the students brought their decision to the board that they would not participate in games against the towns which wouldn't play us. The board accepted the decision that was made, and then we had the support of everybody and we were all in accord that we should not play those teams, and those games were canceled. I believe that Harrison, Arkansas, was one of them. They all said that they were afraid for us to bring black boys, because in northwest Arkansas we had a small community of blacks. Springdale didn't have any blacks. Rogers didn't have any, . . . I am not sure about Harrison.

We had a black boy in the chorus. I mean they [blacks] were not excluded from anything; they were totally integrated when they came in; of course, it might be easier in a small group.

I: Did you notice any sort of discrimination during class—such as, did you pick teams in physical education for activities?

FM: We counted off, but as well as I remember, the black girls did

very well on the teams and were always very respected. . . . I think
that [integration] was just the law of the land and we moved in that
direction. And we had a unique situation because we had people
going to different schools and we didn't have to bring the black students all in at the same time.

I: Why do you think that the integration went so smoothly here?

FM: Because so few black students were involved. Mrs. [Louise]
Bell was always prepared for situations and able to anticipate problems, so I think she is totally responsible for the fact that everything
went so smoothly. . . . It could have been done poorly, I guess. After
we integrated, we could have divided the feelings that people had if
we had decided to leave the black players at home and go ahead and
play those teams.

I: So how long did you teach?

FM: I taught from 1953 to 1956. I had taught from '43 to '46. In
1943 Mr. [Virgil] Blossom had hired me to set up the physical education department for girls. Then I taught for three years, got married. Then I went back ten years later and taught three or more
years.

I: Then you were on the school board?

FM: From 1967–1986. Is that nineteen years? It is a long story why
I stayed so long. That was six terms. My friends began calling me
Feriba Faubus. . . . I went to high school and college here, and I
have always been interested in education. Now, I am on the Fayetteville Public School Education Foundation. I have always been interested in Fayetteville's public school system, in public education.
America has benefited from public education. Unless we educate all
students as well as we can, our problems as a country will be much
worse than they are.

HARRY VANDERGRIFF

Harry Vandergriff, a native of Van Buren, Arkansas, served as a teacher, coach, and administrator in the Fayetteville schools prior to becoming superintendent of schools. In 1954-55 he was the Fayetteville High School football coach.

HARRY VANDERGRIFF: I got two [Fayetteville High School] annuals out. And I was surprised in the 1954 annual that it didn't have much about the integration. There just wasn't anything in it. There were a few pictures of black kids, just a few, and that year there were no athletes. Most of the black kids that came as athletes came the next year and as sophomores that next year. There were one or two when I looked through. So, they integrated that year ['55]. When I got this annual out, looking back, I was really disappointed, [looks at annual] see this says, "This is the first year that Fayetteville High had integration." But that isn't right, but that is all that it says about it. And looking back, that was really a very important decision that they made and a very important time, and they just didn't say anything about it.

INTERVIEWER: Your position at the time was what?

HV: I was the football coach. A man named Glen Stokenberry and I were the coaches. He was the basketball coach. And I think that we may have been the only two coaches at the time.

I: So, you didn't integrate the athletic program until the year after integration, is that right?

HV: Yes, that's right. The first year that we integrated, I'm not sure, but I think there were just a handful of kids, and most of them were girls. In fact, they all may have been, I'm not sure.

I: How many students did the high school have at this time?

HV: We had probably in the tenth to twelfth grades about seven hundred or so.

I: And how many black students came, do you remember?

HV: Not very many. Seemed to me that the first year there were only a handful. [refers to the school board minutes] See, this was May 1954, so the kids started that fall, the fall of '54. And there weren't very many that year. This yearbook is the fall of '55 and that was when we decided that we would cancel football games or other athletic events if they didn't want to play with our black athletes.

I: I heard that you actually asked the players how they felt about cancelling these games.

HV: My recollection of it is that Mrs. [Louise] Bell, the principal, had a meeting of the faculty, and as I have said my memory is fuzzy. I am not sure if all of the faculty was at the meeting, or just some of the faculty, but there was a group of faculty and some students and we met and discussed about the athletes playing or not, and we all agreed unanimously. I don't believe anybody objected. We said if the black kids would be part of the teams, and if schools refused to play us then we just wouldn't play. And so that's what we did, as I recall. The first year we had Fort Smith, Harrison, and Russellville, Arkansas—all three of those schools refused to play us because of the black kids.

I: How many schools did you play?

HV: I believe that year we only wound up playing seven football games, I will look at the yearbook and see. I do remember that we had a call from an all-black high school over in Tulsa that wanted to play us. But we couldn't because of scheduling—they couldn't play when we could play. This is a '56 yearbook. Well, we had eight games. We played everybody around here—Siloam Springs, Subiaco, Rogers, Springdale, Van Buren, and Huntsville in Arkansas, and Springfield and Joplin in Missouri. So, we had eight games.

I remember Van Buren. They were concerned more about the newspaper, the press. So, the coach at Van Buren . . . just would never say whether they were going to play us or not. The press kept calling and wanting to know if we were going to play, and kept calling us and we would say, "Well, we don't know." He wouldn't say yes, and he wouldn't say no, but we had them on the schedule. And the night of the ballgame, here they came, so we played. He was afraid that there would be a bunch of publicity about it. There was a bunch of publicity out of Fort Smith about it, negative publicity about the black kids, and he was afraid that that would happen to Van Buren.

One of the sad things about the whole thing, looking back, is about the state athletic association. Back in those days, they had an association of schools that elected representatives from the schools and they made policies, just like a school board. But the director, Johnnie Burnett, was pretty autocratic and whatever he decided is what the board agreed to. He ruled that year that the teams that had black kids would have to forfeit ballgames if the team that they were playing refused to play against blacks. In other words, blacks could not participate. Period. And so in basketball, if there was a basketball tournament, if they objected to black kids, then we just couldn't play in the tournament. And they always had a state tournament, and we couldn't go to it because of the black kids. And track, we always went to the state track meet, but we couldn't take black kids to the state track meet.

I: How long did this last?

HV: That just lasted one year, if I remember right, maybe two, because the courts got involved. The athletic association realized that it couldn't get by with that.

I: Did that come from the membership, or was it mainly Johnnie Burnett's thing?

HV: Well, back in those days, Johnnie Burnett ruled—now, his executive committee may have approved it, but Johnnie, whatever Johnnie said, that's what happened.

I: I want to go back for a minute to what you said about the coach in Van Buren worrying about the press. Was it a case of being fearful of any publicity, or did you get a sense that the newspapers had an interest in this one way or another?

HV: Van Buren didn't have a lot of blacks, but they had more than we had, and I think that they were fearful that they, because of this business with Fayetteville, might be forced to integrate sooner than they wanted to. I think that was part of it.

I: Mr. Vandergriff, what impact did integration have on athletics at Fayetteville? Was that a factor in the acceptance of the integration or not?

HV: No. I don't think it had any measurable impact at all. I don't think the teams were better or worse or anything. The kids, the Fayetteville kids got along real well, blacks and whites. They just—I guess, I don't know whether it was the novelty of it or what, but the white kids just took the black kids in, and I think that the most popular kids on the teams were always the blacks.

I: Did the fact that the black students participated in athletics have anything to do with their being accepted in the school community?

HV: I think so. I think it did. But now there were some that didn't participate in athletics. And the girls, it seemed to me the girls were not really as much a part of the school community as the boy athletes. Now, there was one black kid—his name was Preston Lackey. Preston was a student, but he was not an athlete. And he seemed to get along real well. A lot of the black people, back in those days, were domestics. They worked for families in town, and the families got to know them real well, and I think that helped integration too. These white families knew the kids and knew the mother and the father, and I think that—they were friendly—and I think that helped integration, especially since there were so few of them.

I: What do you remember about the decision to integrate? How did the community react? Was there any opposition?

HV: Back then, the coaches would go to businesses around town and ask them to buy season football tickets just to help financially support the schools, and I recall one very prominent man who had always bought a block of tickets to help, and when I went to talk to him, he was just irate. He would never buy another ticket for a Fayetteville High School ballgame and would never go to another Fayetteville High ballgame. But there were very few of those.

And the players themselves. They just got along beautifully. The student body, I think they took the black kids in and just brought them in and treated them royally just because they thought that was the thing to do. I think that some of the most popular kids we had in school were black.

We had a boy named William Hayes that played football, and that year, 1955, he was a sophomore, and he had never played before so he really wasn't a real help to the football team. But the kids teased him and played with him, tickled him. I remember the football team would get him down and tickle him and he would laugh and carry on. And at school and the pep rallies and things when he was introduced, well, everybody just loved him, they called him Bull. And he wound up a real good football player by the time he graduated. He got a scholarship to the University of Nebraska to play football. But he got his knee hurt as a freshman over there and finally wound up, well I think he wound up playing in Pittsburg, Kansas, at Pittsburg State. He wound up as a director of a boys' club and then died of sickle-cell anemia when he was real young. But he was really one of the nicest kids.

I don't know if you knew Mr. [M. O.] Ramay, who was principal of Hillcrest Junior High, and then he became principal of Ramay Junior High—the board named it after him later—but Mr. Ramay was pretty old then and he was a pretty gruff kind of fellow and very dignified; and there was one boy named Harold Hayes, a black kid who played basketball. He was a good basketball player. He befriended Mr. Ramay, and Mr. Ramay couldn't help but like him. He would come up and hug him, that sort of thing. But he [Harold Hayes] was another tragedy. He went to Joplin Junior College and was on the basketball and golf teams and they were going to a golf match one day, just some kids in the car, and they stopped at a strip mine of some sort to swim, and he drowned.

But I can also remember, this happened a few times, more in basketball than football because most of our trips were short trips. Some of the restaurants that we tried to eat at would not let the black kids in, so we would refuse to eat there. But that didn't last very long.

I: Was it the kind of thing where you would have to go in before time and inform them that—

HV: That's right. Yeah. We tried to make reservations to eat before we left. It happened more than once. Now, part of the time, you know, we'd call ahead, a few days ahead, and make arrangements, and we'd tell them we had blacks. And if they said no, why then that was the end of it. Go someplace else.

I: One of the things that struck me was the matter-of-fact way in which this integration was carried out.

HV: Now, school board meetings—one thing you have to remember back then, school board meetings were always held in private. When I say private, what they did here, and I assume they did in lots of other places, the school board would get together at a restaurant up town at noon and have their meeting. The press or nobody else was present. Nobody even attempted to be present, and evidently didn't want to be present. And then after the meeting the superintendent would call the press if he thought there was something important that they needed to know. Otherwise, there wasn't anything in the press.

And so if it had been like it is now, even under the same circumstances, there would have been a big issue made out of it in the press. See, since it was so closed and everything, it was just, as far as they [school board] were concerned, it was a matter that had to be done. It was a done deal before anybody knew about it, and I think that contributed to the ease with which it happened.

I: You said that the student body was real accepting of the black kids. Was the community very segregated?

HV: No, we didn't have any real overt hostility. There were people that were hostile in a way, but there wasn't much bad publicity about it. We just didn't have trouble between blacks and whites.

Later on we had a little trouble. I don't remember the year or years but it seemed to me like it was in the late '60s and early '70s when for the first time we had interracial dating, but it was always in every case that I know of, it was black boys dating white girls. The trouble we had was the black girls resented the white girls. So, we had a few fights and things of that nature, but it was between girls. And it was always resolved. And a lot of the kids, the white and black too, didn't much like interracial dating. The white girls that dated the black boys were pretty well ostracized by the rest of the kids.

I: Do you know what precipitated the decision by the school board to go ahead and integrate?

HV: Yes, I know part of it. The black high school kids were sent first to Fort Smith schools, and the Fayetteville school district paid for them to go there. Evidently, they had to pay for the students to live down there, and Fort Smith High School got so crowded that they couldn't send students there anymore. So, they started sending students to Hot Springs. And then Hot Springs became crowded. So, they [Fayetteville] just had to integrate. So, really they were forced to do this. Either that or find someone else to take them. One of the things is that there were very few blacks, and so they didn't have many black high schoolers. Of course, in those days there were an awful lot of dropouts, black and white. The dropout rate was much higher then than now.

We had an elementary school here for a long time called the Lincoln School. It was over behind the court house up on top of that hill. They have an apartment complex there now. And I don't remember the year, but it was several years after [1954] that before we integrated the elementary school.

I remember when I was assistant superintendent talking to the black people in their community to get their opinion about where they wanted to send their kids [to elementary school]. We told them we would send them—we could put an equal number of blacks in each of the schools or we could send them to the closest schools or what. And they wanted us to send them to the closest schools, and the two closest ones were Washington and Jefferson, and then as time went on, black families moved about in Fayetteville and we had black kids all around.

I: It strikes me as strange that they were so quick to integrate the high school and so slow about integrating the other schools here in Fayetteville.

HV: Now, I know that when it came time to integrate the elementary school (I don't know when this happened), I was assistant superintendent. There were quite a few people in town who were pushing to integrate, get the black elementary school integrated with the other schools. And one fellow that was very active in those days in trying to get this to happen was a professor at the University named Phil Bashor.

I: Do you have any perspective on why there was such a gap in time between the integration of the high school and then the other schools?

HV: Yes, I think that I do. They integrated the high school because they had to. They were sending high school kids to Fort Smith, and Fort Smith told them that they couldn't send any more kids down there. So they sent some to Hot Springs, and this source was drying up also. So, they had to provide for the high school kids here. And there weren't enough students to have a black high school, so it was a necessity. And see, nobody else in this whole area had black kids except Fayetteville.

I: You mean in the community or in the schools?

HV: In the community. There were not any black people. They used to say that Springdale had a rule that black people couldn't spend the night in Springdale, and I suppose that's probably true. There just were no blacks, period. And so there was no place to put them, to send the kids. So it was just absolutely necessary to integrate the high school.

I: How did you feel about the integration, personally?

HV: I was all for it. It was fine with me. I am from Van Buren, Arkansas, originally, and my father worked on the railroad for years, and of course, the decision was made to integrate by the board, and as a coach I didn't have any input in it, didn't even know it was happening until it was announced. I do remember the head-lines in the newspaper. It said, "Fayetteville High School Integrates, Including Athletics." That was the headline. At any rate, my daddy, he thought I was the one who caused it all and he was not very pleased with me. And for three or four or five years—well, there were two things he was mad at me about, one was the integration and the other was because I got a crew cut. Over the years, he was fussing about it, and one day we were talking, and as a railroader he worked with black people all the time. So, one day we were talking and I said, "Don't you work with black people?" He said, "Yes." I said, "How do you get along?" He said, "Just fine. But I don't go home with them at night." I said that the black kids and white kids don't go home together either. "They are like you; they work together during the day and go their own way at night." And he said that he hadn't thought about it that way. From that time on he was happy and supportive. . . .

I: So, there really weren't any problems of any kind?

HV: No, the problems we had were problems with other schools. When the black kids played football, the other teams tended to sort of single them out to try and hurt them. And you could sort of hear the people talking about the blacks. But it worked out all right because none of them ever really got hurt. But the other kids did their best to try and protect them. The white kids really protected those black kids.

And I remember that Bentonville had a few, very few; one family is all it was. That came along a lot later, actually. But none of the other schools around here had any. I think Springdale has a few now, but no athletes. But I guess that is kind of hard on the black kids to be the only ones among all the whites. . . .

I: Why do you think the integration was so successful here?

HV: I think that Fayetteville is a unique place. Fayetteville is more, for lack of a better term, more cosmopolitan than most of the towns this size, because the University is here, and we have profes-sors and families from all over the country. In fact, all over the world, I guess, and lots and lots of people that live in Fayetteville are people that came here from everywhere, and so that makes it differ-ent to start with. And I think that Fayetteville is not like the Deep South. In fact, you don't have to go very far to find towns that are very prejudiced toward anybody other than themselves. But Fayette-ville's not like that. We are just different. And we had, I guess, probably 2 percent black, something like that. And you could hardly find a black kid in the school. You'd have maybe ten blacks and eight hundred whites. You know, it just wasn't a problem. And as I say, the white kids just took the black kids in: it was pretty nice, kind of natural. They thoroughly enjoyed the black kids.

I am just pleased that you all are doing this. I got the yearbook out, and it really shows how unimportant the integration was to the people of that time, because they made mention of it, and that's all. You know, there's nothing except one little statement in the yearbook. And you know, looking back, it was a very momentous occasion for the schools to be integrated. And there was nothing. And the newspapers were the same way. There just wasn't a whole lot.

I: Did you find that because you were a coach and because blacks were successful in athletics that you developed a kind of better relationship with members of the black community than you might have otherwise?

HV: Well, I think that is probably true.

I: That you occupy a somewhat higher position in their eyes?

HV: I think that may be, especially since we treated the black kids like we did. Well, there was a letter to the editor that sums up a lot of people's feelings. We'd had a pep rally. When the black kids were introduced, the applause was greater than when the white kids were introduced. And they were really brought into the mainstream.

BEN WINBORN AND
MILDRED BAILEY WINBORN

Ben Winborn, a native of Alma, Arkansas, was a teacher and coach at Fayetteville High School, and Mrs. Winborn (Mildred Bailey Winborn) was secretary to the principal, Mrs. Louise Bell. Mr. Winborn was later an administrator in the Fayetteville public school system. He and Mrs. Winborn currently reside in Fayetteville.

INTERVIEWER: Mrs. Winborn, what was your position at the time of the integration?

MILDRED BAILEY WINBORN: In 1953, I was the secretary for Mrs. [Louise] Bell who was the principal of the high school. The high school at that time had about five hundred students.

I: What about you Mr. Winborn? And how did you feel about the decision to integrate?

BEN WINBORN: Well, I came back here in the summer of 1954. I just thought that after the *Brown* decision was made that everyone would have black kids in schools everywhere. I gave very little thought to objections to the integration. I know of very little opposition locally. There was one real estate man here that said that the highways would just be black with them coming in here to go to school since we were integrating, but no one moved in as far as I know.

At that time, the school board was very unified and there was never a nay vote. They were not autocratic, but they didn't mind telling you when you made a mistake.

Everyone realized that there might be problems between the students in school, but little happened. The [swimming] pool in town was not integrated, and the sports outside of the high school were not either. There were very little city sports in those days.

MW: There were only three or four girls the first year. Mrs. Bell, the principal, stayed very close to the black students. She depended on Preston Lackey to tell her about any problems. She acted like a counselor for all of them

I: Mr. Winborn, you were the basketball coach, is that right?

BW: Yes. Each year we would have about one hundred players to try out for the basketball team, and we would only keep about twenty-four to twenty-five kids. No blacks came out that first year. Black kids had little opportunity to learn basketball then. No playgrounds were kept up for them. After I left, they took one of the black kids to a tournament and the whole team was not allowed to play in the tournament. I believe that was in 1958. The state ruled that a school with black players would forfeit or leave them home.

I: How did you feel about the problems you had in athletics?

BW: I thought that the decision to integrate was the right one. And the few problems that we incurred in athletics were wrong. Other school people thought we were creating problems by bringing our black students. But we really would have created problems if we did not include the blacks on the teams.

I remember once we got a phone call from Harrison threatening violence if we brought our black player, William Hayes. I remember that the boys just grouped around him and kept him away from the crowd. People made comments to William from the stands at Harrison. I don't remember a problem of this type elsewhere. After the problems in Little Rock, things were worse for the black kids here.

I: The blacks were accepted in athletics. How about the other activities or groups at the school?

BW: Most of the activities were exclusive groups; that is, they elected their members. I know that the Key Club did it that way. They are a high school group sponsored by the Kiwanis Club. These groups kept a lot of kids out, not just the blacks.

Part of the problem was that there often were scholastic requirements to be a part of these clubs. And the blacks just didn't seem to be ready scholastically. It was not a matter of intelligence, just scholastics. I remember that they had terrific penmanship but were weak in other basic skills. You see, the black students did not have many teaching aids and the staff that the other schools had. So, when they got to the high school, they just were not ready, scholastically, especially the boys.

I think that Fayetteville had one of the top ten schools in the whole state. And they had a really strong school board and well-qualified teachers. Plus the students, with the University here, were very interested in scholastic attainment.

I: Why do you think that the process went so smoothly here as opposed to other places?

BW: There was good community support, although we were not that progressive. We really integrated because it was cheaper. And the staff of the school just wouldn't put up with any problems. I know that I wouldn't. I wouldn't stand for anything being said or done against those black kids, or any other disadvantaged kids.

I think that the whole integration process was delayed because President [Dwight] Eisenhower didn't put up a strong enough hand. No one came up with a plan.

JUANITA CAUDLE

Juanita Caudle, a native of Washington County, Arkansas, and a teacher for many years in Fayetteville, was principal of the town's Washington Elementary School in 1954. (Mrs. Margaret Stephan participated in this interview also.)

INTERVIEWER: I wanted to get your impressions of this whole series of events that took place in '54.

JUANITA CAUDLE: Well, I think the beginning of the Fayetteville schools was interesting because the colored people had a free school here before the white people did. There was a colored school—the colored school was built, and it is still standing on East Lafayette [Street]. The first black school. Some ladies from the North, a group, built a school for the colored people here. And now, at that time, there was not a school for the white children, so I understand. But that is still standing, and they used it as a school until they built Lincoln. . . .

I: Mrs. Caudle, what was your position—at the time of the racial integration of the schools, you were the—

JC: Well, now, in integration, the high school—well, at first, they had the colored school, and they didn't have a public school here for the children. Then they built two, just two schools. There was Washington School, which was north of Center Street, and Jefferson School, which was south of Center Street. Now, that's when I came as principal. Stella Hall was principal of the south school, and I was principal of Washington School. And at that time we just had the two public schools. And the colored school, it was Lincoln. . . . It was on Fletcher. They had two colored teachers and about forty students. But before integration, we brought them into the public schools and everything. For instance, we'd have a program. We'd ask Miss [Minnie] Dawkins [principal at Lincoln] and the children, and they'd use the school buses. I think we just had two. They'd use the bus to bring the children to Washington School when we had a little program.

I: Black students?

JC: The black students. Now that was—it wasn't integration, but—they brought them to our program. Now, when Miss Dawkins would have a program, she would invite maybe the sixth grade or seventh in Washington School over to Lincoln, and we'd go over there.

MARGARET STEPHAN: Go back and forth for programs.

JC: Back and forth. Now, she—she came to our faculty meetings—when we had principal meetings on Saturdays, she would come, and we accepted her just as one of the other of the faculty. And then when we had integration, when the law was passed for integration—Oh, yes, I want to say something else. Fayetteville did something that I doubt that any other school—I know no other school in Arkansas and probably the United States did. When the children finished the eighth grade, there wasn't any colored school for them to go to. And the Fayetteville school district paid their tuition and board in Fort Smith or Pine Bluff; I guess it was Pine Bluff.

I: Hot Springs also.

JC: It may have been Hot Springs. They paid their tuition and also their board. Now, the Fayetteville schools did that. Now, they didn't have many, maybe three, maybe four. So it didn't break them. And they usually stayed with some of their relatives or friends, and their board didn't cost them too much. But they did that voluntarily. And so that is the way our first colored people in Fayetteville were educated. Then when integration came along, I guess [Superintendent] Virgil Blossom was still here. The faculty—I mean, the administration or the principals and Virgil Blossom—we met with the colored people. And he said, "Now, what do you want to do? How do you want your children integrated into the public schools? We want to do what you want to do, what you want." And they said that they voted their children to go to the school closest to where they lived. He gave them a choice, said, "Now, we could put all the children in one school or you can go [close to] where you live." Well, at that time, the colored people in Arkansas all lived over in what we called "nigger town." I wouldn't call it "nigger town" today.

JC: But it was on—

MS: Center Street—they were a community.

JC: They were a community. Mr. Blossom said, "Now what do you want to do?" And they talked it over, and they took a vote, and they said, "We want to go to the school . . . [near where] we live. We don't want to all go together." And it so happened that every one of them either lived in Jefferson School, where Miss Stella Hall was principal, or in Washington School, where I was principal. They divided them about fifty-fifty.

I: How many people are we talking about?

JC: Colored children, about fifty, I would say.

I: And they divided it about twenty-five–twenty-five.

JC: Twenty-five in each school.

I: What grades were involved?

JC: The grades—it was elementary school—and I believe it was an eight-four plan then [Elementary school was first through eighth grade; high school was ninth through twelfth].

I: Eight-four.

JC: Eight-four. That's before we went into the six-three-three [Elementary school is now first through sixth; grades seven through nine are junior high; and high school is tenth through twelfth grade]. And we had just the two elementary schools. Stella Hall was principal of one, and I was principal of the other one. And that was while Virgil Blossom was here . . . we didn't have any problems with integrating in Fayetteville. We did just what they wanted, and we were fortunate in the fact that they—about half of them lived in one district and half of them in another.

I: Mrs. Caudle, I've asked Dr. Stephan this and Mrs. Stephan. I want to ask you, why was it that there was so little trouble here and so much trouble other places?

JC: I think it was the fact that we went to the people. The first thing we did was have all of the colored people come to a meeting. And the principals or administrators of the Fayetteville schools were there. And they asked them, "What do you want to do? How do you want to do it? Do you want your children all to go to one school? Or do you want them to go close to where they live?" And Fayetteville was fortunate in the fact that Center Street divided our white children. And when we extended Center Street through the colored population, it divided them almost half and half. And then, at that time, the real estate people had gotten the people—had made the impression with people in Fayetteville that Washington School in the north part of town was a better school. Now, that was not true.

I: Now, this is where you were or where Miss Hall was?

JC: I was over there. Stella Hall was at Jefferson. But the real estate people, when they'd start to sell property—well, [they said] you want in Washington School because that's the best school. . . .

MS: That was the story, yes.

JC: But it wasn't. I think, if anything, the school board tried to place the strongest teachers down in the south part of town because they knew the children in the north part of town had more advantages.

I: Why did the white community cooperate so well here as opposed to other places?

JC: Well, I think that—well, first place, we asked them [the black community] what they wanted. We went to them. We didn't say, "Now, we're going to do this, and we're going to stick it down your throat. We're going to do this." But we said, "What do you want to do? The law says we must integrate. Now how do you want it? If you want your children all to go to one school, that's what we will do." Maybe it was the type of colored people that we had. They said, "We want our children to go according to where we live." And at that time they didn't live all over Fayetteville as they do today.

I: What was it about the white community that made the transition easier here than it was other places? You didn't seem to have much problem with the whites either.

JC: Yes, well, I don't know. Maybe it was because we didn't have too many, maybe. There's always been labor—good work for them to do here. Many of them worked for people at the University, and there's been employment for them. And I think we just had—they have lived a better—

I: Economically, they've been better off?

JC: Economically, don't you think that's true?

MS: Yes, and some of those people worked for some of these people on the school board.

JC: Yes. Well, that was true.

MS: Well, they knew them a little bit.

JC: Now, you see, the black people—now, I taught in Forrest City seven years.

I: A very different situation?

JC: A different situation entirely. I lived on a plantation, and they grew good cotton at that time. Well, in just a few years, many professional colored people of different races moved to Fayetteville because of the University. And their children went to the public schools, and I think that had a lot to do with it.

I: So the fact that the University was here—

JC: The University was here, and many educators. And then, of course, integration came on, and the University began to have colored teachers, and not only colored teachers but people from other countries, foreign countries. And they sent their children to the public schools. It wasn't, well, there weren't private schools to send them to. Of course, Fayetteville was different from a lot of the schools in Arkansas.

I: That's what I wanted to get at. What is that difference?

JC: Well, I think there's more professional [black] people here. And even most of the farmers, you don't have sharecroppers. They own their own farms. They just are economically better off.

I: Do you recall any kind of active campaign or anything by the churches or by civic organizations?

JC: No. Now, they helped us. For instance, in the beginning of the schools, we only got our money to run the public schools from a tax on land. And that, of course, soon became a poor way to get your money. And we worked very hard to get the first sales tax, a 2 percent sales tax, and it went—I think all of it—went to the public schools. But then as they needed other money, they increased the sales tax and gave part of it to the Fayetteville schools but used part of it for other purposes.

I: What about the relationship between the whites and the black students in the school itself when integration came?

JC: Well, I don't think there was any trouble. Of course, I think part of it, now, I don't know whether I told you. We did something by sending these children off that wanted to go on to high school. And, you know, the colored teachers and we—well, the school, encouraged . . . those colored children to go to high school. First, by providing them an opportunity to go. I know there wasn't another district in Arkansas, and maybe in the United States, that paid for their tuition, boarded them, bought their books, to go to high school because they didn't furnish a high school. We didn't have one. We didn't have to.

MS: Mrs. Caudle, don't you think Minnie Dawkins had a lot to do with these people going on? She was a terrific person.

JC: Miss Dawkins was wonderful—she was a colored teacher. Miss Dawkins was principal of the colored school, and we accepted her in our school meetings, principal meetings. If we had a dinner, Miss Dawkins was invited. Any time there was anything for any of the principals in Fayetteville, Miss Dawkins was there.

MS: Well, she must have inspired those kids to go on and their parents to let them go.

JC: Yes, that's what she did. She [encouraged] the children and their parents to give them an opportunity to go. Now, when we were paying them to go to Fort Smith, even before—some years maybe you'd have one or two more go on to high school.

I: But students were pretty well accepted in your school, the black students by the white students?

JC: Now, you're asking me a question that I can't answer.

I: As far as you were able to observe.

JC: Well, what I mean, did I teach after integration? I guess I did.

MS: Well, you were a principal.

JC: I didn't have any trouble. I think they were accepted, and we were always very proud of some of the records that some of our students in high school made in athletics especially. I think they got recognition. Now, the high school—and, of course, I think there is where your problems would come because of encouraging them to go on to the University. And the University cooperated with us, with the schools here, encouraging. And we took them—oh, any time they had anything to do with the University, we could get the school buses if we wanted to take a child over there—a group of children over there—the school administrators were very nice, and we could get a school bus. They'd send them transportation. And we gave them an opportunity to see things at the University, to give the children a desire to want to go on. The school board gave us good guidance. There wasn't any opposition or anything, and they kept the principals well informed, and then the fact that we took the colored people and asked them, let them have a part in it. We just didn't try to cram something down their throats.

I: Now, I know having been a principal that you're the first person that people from the community come to when they have a problem. Did you get any kind of negative feedback from the community or concerns from the community when this process was taking place, from white parents who were worried about the effect it was going to have on the school?

JC: I don't think that I did. I don't recall any. It just seemed a natural thing here. And I think we had a very understanding board. . . . At that time, we had businessmen in Fayetteville on the school board.

MS: Yes, they were on the school board.

JC: They were on the school board, and they ran it in a very businesslike way, from finances. And we had nothing to do with that. And they kind of left the administration of the schools—

MS: To run the schools.

JC: To run the schools. And they ran the finances. They really did. And now—and then, too—they had the administrators come to the school board meetings, many of them, especially when they were planning and dividing the money up for next year. And when they'd have to maybe cut something out or we'd want something they couldn't afford, they would ask us about it.

I: But you don't recall any instances of angry parents coming to the school and saying—expressing some concern about what was going to happen when these black students came in? You know, that kind of thing is very common all over the South. You don't recall that?

JC: No, I don't recall. I think the fact that—we would look forward to when the black children, the people at Washington School—when Miss Dawkins would bring her children over there to have their little plays and all, why, we just—

MS: Made a big thing out of it.

JC: And Miss Dawkins made a big thing when we went over there. That was just something special to go over and see—

MS: And all that preceded the integration. Right, she [Miss Dawkins] was a remarkable woman.

JC: Well, in fact, Miss Dawkins stayed through integration, I think. I'm sure she did. But as far as I remember, I was in Washington School and got half of the children. Now, when I went to Leverett—I had both schools during the Depression. And then when they got some more money, why they took—that's the way they saved money during the Depression was giving a principal [two schools]. They split me. They gave me two secretaries. In other words, they could hire a secretary cheaper than they could hire a teacher. And they gave me two schools and two secretaries.

I: Now, when integration took place, what happened to the principal and teachers of the black school?

JC: They were taken into the schools. They gave one—now, that's another thing. There were two teachers. And they put the two in Washington School. Washington and Leverett.

I: The principal at that time, you think, was Miss Dawkins?

JC: Miss Dawkins was principal of the black school.

I: What happened to her when the integration—

JC: It could be that she got the offer of a job in Little Rock.

MS: I don't think she ever went into one of these schools, did she?

JC: I don't believe she did. I think she got a job in Little Rock. I believe that's when we lost Miss Dawkins. But it just seemed like it went on naturally, and I believe it was because of the board handling it the way they did. They said, "Well, what do you want to do." They didn't say, "Now this is what we're going to do." And we just didn't know. Now, Virgil Blossom was here, and he went to Little Rock. And he thought he could do the same thing down there.

Henderson School. *Courtesy of the Washington County Historical Society, Fayetteville*

Lincoln School. *Courtesy of Ms. Thelma Thomason*

Fayetteville High School. *From* The Amethyst, 1964 *(Fayetteville High School Yearbook)*

Mrs. Louise Bell, Principal, Fayetteville High School. *From* The Amethyst, 1955 *(Fayetteville High School Yearbook)*

Harry Vandergriff, Teacher and Football Coach, Fayetteville High School. *From* The Amethyst, 1964 *(Fayetteville High School Yearbook)*

Wayne White, Superintendent of Fayetteville Schools. *From* The Amethyst, 1964 *(Fayetteville High School Yearbook)*

The Fayetteville School Board, 1954. l. to r.: William C. Morton, Henry Shreve, Hal C. Douglas, Ray Adams, Haskell Utley, and Clark C. McClinton. *From* The Amethyst, 1955 *(Fayetteville High School Yearbook)*

Lodene Deffebaugh,
Activist in behalf of
desegregation.
*Courtesy of Ms.
Deffebaugh*

Hal C. Douglas,
Secretary of the
Fayetteville School
Board, 1954. *Courtesy
of Ms. Jacqueline
Douglas*

Fayetteville High School Students. *From* The Los Angeles Times

Preparing African-
American Elementary
Students for
Integrated Schools,
Tutor Lorraine Bashor
and Her Son. *Courtesy
of Ms. Lorraine Bashor*

Fayetteville School
Board, 1964. Top,
l. to r.: Henry Shreve,
George Tharel. Middle,
l. to r.: Hal C. Douglas,
William Morton.
Bottom, l. to r.: Haskell
Utley, Richard Walden.
From The Amethyst, 1964
*(Fayetteville High
School Yearbook)*

PART TWO

PUBLIC SCHOOL

STUDENTS

DAVID McCLINTON

David McClinton, a prominent businessman, was a Fayetteville High School student in 1954–55. He is the son of Clark C. McClinton, who was a member of the school board.

INTERVIEWER: You were there in the Fayetteville High School a year before it integrated. So, you were there the year that the black students started school.

DAVID McCLINTON: It was integrated at the start of my junior year [1954].

I: Do you remember how you found out about the decision?

DM: I can remember very well how I found out about it. That summer, the phone would ring, and my dad [Clark C. McClinton, school board member] would refuse to talk to anyone who would not identify themselves. He would be talking to someone, and all of the sudden he would just hang up because they wouldn't identify themselves. That summer, I learned that you don't talk to someone on the telephone unless they will tell you who they are. He refused to talk to anyone who wouldn't. But that's the way that I found out that the schools were going to be integrated—with the telephone calls.

I: Did it change anything for you at school?

DM: Absolutely not. Here's what else I remember about that. The first day, rumors were going around that there was going to be a bunch of people there, and they were going to blockade the thing and no [black] students were going to get in. Some of us decided that that was not going to happen, and we were going to be there and we were going to walk those people in the door. And I got to school and went down to the end where the gym is; that's where they were going to come in. And I got there just as they came in. There was one person, a female who was standing across the street on the sidewalk with a sign, and she yelled something, and she was the only person that I remember seeing protest. Preston Lackey was the black student, the man that year. I enjoyed being around him; we were friends. His race didn't mean one thing to me.

I: We have generally found that everything went so smoothly. Now, we are wondering if and why that was the case.

DM: I think that there was more than one reason, and I don't know how they play, but first it was done real quiet, before any opposition could build up. Secondly, we have so few blacks in this area. I have known blacks all my life, . . . well, there are so few of them. I think that those two things are why it was done so easily.

I: So, that first day you remember one woman who was opposed to it.

DM: One woman. White shirt, long dark hair, dark complexion, white sign pole, I don't have any memory of what it said. But I remember seeing one person standing up on that wall. And she yelled something, and I can't remember what, and we went back inside the school.

I: Do you remember any incidents between a white and a black student?

DM: Absolutely not. I mean, I think had there been any, I would remember them. But it wasn't there. If it happened, I didn't know about it. . . . There were no incidents.

I: Tell me about Mrs. [Louise] Bell as principal.

DM: Oh, I love her to death. I would do anything in the world for her, but even now, I can shake in my boots just thinking about her. I mean, Mrs. Bell was tough. I mean she was a strong person . . . and I love her to this day . . .

ROBERTA LACKEY MORGAN

Roberta Lackey Morgan, born near Fayetteville, had lived in the city for nine years when she entered Fayetteville High School as one of the first African-American students. She and her family currently reside in Fayetteville.

INTERVIEWER:: What are your recollections of 1954 and how the change, how integration, affected your life?

ROBERTA LACKEY MORGAN: That's hard. I remember why they integrated. I think it was about seven of us; five or seven, I can't remember. Seemed like it was seven because it was the biggest class they'd had in the history [of Lincoln School]. There was seven of us coming out that year, out of the ninth grade. And my brother and my husband, who was Bobby Morgan, and Peggy Taylor. And I think there were about five more. Let's see, my brother and his friend and Bobby. Bobby had a high school football scholarship, so he went to the black school in Hot Springs because he had a full scholarship.

I: Now, your brother went there too, right?

RM: Yes.

I: So you were, you weren't Roberta Morgan, of course, then; you were—

RM: Lackey. And so they went there, my husband and another fellow, to play football. And Preston just went because they were close friends and he wanted to go, but he had to pay out of his pocket for living facilities. I think the school paid tuition. Let's see, it was about—best I could remember—there was one girl that graduated in his class.

I: That leaves him [Roberta Morgan's brother] and one other black student in the junior class, and I believe he said maybe five sophomores, so that would be about what your memory of it is.

RM: Yes, I've lost track, really. But I remember some of them were already going to Fort Smith. They'd gone to Fort Smith—five or seven, I can't remember—but the school board was paying tuition for them also.

I: How did that work, Mrs. Morgan? Did that money come through you or just go from the district to the district?

RM: District to the other district.

I: You didn't ever—you didn't see the money.

RM: No, and let's see. The only time they got to come home from school that whole year was Christmas vacation. . . . I don't remember who paid for it for them to come home, but, you know, they were down there for the whole year. Like I say, only time they got to go home was Christmas, I guess, before school was out.

I: What were your plans before all this came about? Were your plans to go to Hot Springs too?

RM: Yes—no, Fort Smith, somewhere. It didn't make any difference. In fact, I was banking on it. I really did want to go.

I: You were looking forward to going down there.

RM: Yes.

I: Do you remember when you first learned that the Supreme Court had made this ruling [in the *Brown* case] and that you would be going to what had been a previously all-white school here in Fayetteville? Do you remember when you found out about that and how you felt?

RM: Well, I kind of dreaded it, you know. Really because I didn't know. I really didn't know how it would go. Being the first ones—I wasn't looking forward to being the first ones. But it went OK. I was kind of let down, but, you know, I accepted it because at that time it would have been three of us going to high school—my brother and my sister and myself. I don't know if my folks—they couldn't have afforded [for all three children to go to school in Fort Smith or Hot Springs].

I: When did you find out that you would be going to Fayetteville and not to Fort Smith? Do you remember?

RM: Yes, it was, I think, . . . that summer. Didn't have a whole lot of time.

I: Now, you were coming out of the Lincoln School then.

RM: Yes, ninth grade.

I: And were the five of you that were entering the tenth grade, was that the entire ninth-grade class from the Lincoln School the year before?

RM: Yes.

I: That was everybody.

RM: Yes, it was about five or seven of us. I can't remember exactly how many. But there was some of us, plus the ones that were already in Fort Smith, plus the ones that were in Hot Springs.

I: So your family actually made up about half the group of black students that were the first ones to go down there.

RM: Yes.

I: What do you remember about the experience of actually going the first day? Had anyone tried to prepare you for it or tried to help you out at all?

RM: No, we just went in the dark. Nobody prepared us. We didn't have a meeting or anything that I remember. [It was] really a frightening experience, but I don't know why, . . . just being the first ones, I guess.

I: Your brother was talking about going the first day and hoping there wouldn't be a big crowd of people and everything and was very relieved to find out that there wasn't a big mob or anything.

RM: Oh, no, it wasn't a mob or anything like that. Everybody just went about their business. Of course, the reporters were there from *Jet* and all that kind of stuff, newspapers. In fact, I've got a picture somewhere.

I: I've got a picture I want you to look at.

RM: From the *Jet*?

I: No, I think this is from the annual that year. And here's a picture that made a wire service. This was an AP wire photo. Your brother says he thinks you may be in that picture.

RM: Yes. All of us were, see. That's my sister; that's my cousin; that's me. And that was in the *Jet*, too.

I: Was there an article that went with the picture in *Jet*?

RM: I think so.

I: How did that first day go as far as teachers—

RM: Oh, they were—I can't even remember . . . but it went real good. That little girl that's right there in that picture, she helped us.

I: Do you remember what her name was by any chance?

RM: Gosh no, no. I know that she was real close friends.

I: Now, in this picture, she is just sort of showing you around?

RM: Yes.

I: So this was not the first day of school?

RM: Yes, that was the first day. That's when we went to register.

I: And your sister's name was Elnora Lackey.

RM: Elnora Lackey.

I: Her last name is now what?

RM: Jackson.

I: Jackson. And your cousin—

RM: Is Virginia Smith. And she's a Denton.

I: I've heard that name. And you don't remember the girl's name here in the middle.

RM: [Sighs] No, but I remember her because she was one of my good friends.

I: Do you know if she's still in Fayetteville, or do you know where she is now?

RM: No. I can't remember. Seems like her name was Alice Ann— I don't know. I don't remember.

I: I know that's from a long way back. I guess everybody's read stories about how some black students in some places were harassed by other students or people outside the school. Did you experience any of that at all in the school here?

RM: Well, no, because I think the principal was on top of it. I can't remember who the principal was.

I: Mrs. Louise Bell.

RM: Yes, she was real nice. I guess we—they had it under control, I guess. As far as I remember, we only had one incident.

I: What was that? Do you remember?

RM: Yes, we were studying genetics in biology class. And this little old fellow, he wanted to be a redneck, or he was one of those that didn't like the idea [integration] too much, so every chance he got, he'd come out with some racial slurs, nigger this and nigger that. My brother-in-law was one of those who didn't take that. So whenever he did go through a day of that, he'd catch him after school or down there where they played at the game room. He jacked him up, you know, box his head. So we didn't ever go to the principal.

I: Took care of it yourself in other words.

RM: Yes, we took care of ourselves. This particular time we were studying genetics in a biology class, and this kid, same kid, well, he just came out and said, "If a nigger and a white lady got married and had kids, one of them had blue eyes and the other one had brown eyes, . . . what color would their eyes be?" Oh, I just sat there and my head just swelled up. It took every ounce of my being to stay in there. It was in the middle of a class, and we were studying. But it wouldn't have been so bad if he had said black or Negro or anything, but he said, "If a nigger and a white person get married, what color would the eyes be?" So anyway—

I: He said this just to you or out in the—

RM: In the class, just in the class, you know. So I can't remember—I know it was me, and I think it was my sister, because we were all in the same grade. My sister and I were in the same grade. Because back then, you know, you could start [to school] when you were five years old.

I: Right.

RM: Didn't have to have a birth certificate. So—mama put my age up and my sister's up so that we could go [to school] because she was working over on the [University] campus and she didn't have anybody to keep the other kids. Of course, there was some younger ones, but they—I can't remember what they did.

I: So your sister's actually older than you.

RM: No, I'm the oldest. I'm older than she is, yes. But anyway, she maneuvered it some way, and we got in class the same year. But anyway, it was my sister and my cousin. We were all in biology class.

I: How did the teacher react to that? Remember?

RM: She kind of toned it down. She didn't correct him or anything, but she kind of softened it up . . . and just pretended that it didn't happen. But everybody's first instinct was to get up and walk out. But we went on through class and . . . as soon as class was over, we went to the principal's office [and] told her what had happened. I think she called him in there and talked to him. I don't know, but that was all the incident, you know, outward incident that I remember. The other little incidents, we just took care of, of ourselves, you know.

I: Was that early in the year or—

RM: Yes.

I: That was really near the beginning of the school term?

RM: Yes. And after then, we didn't have any more trouble.

I: So that was the exception rather than the rule. That didn't happen often, that kind of thing.

RM: No, not outwardly in the classroom. But it did happen a lot after school, before school, during the noon hour or something like that.

I: Mrs. Morgan, how about your teachers? Do you remember any particular ones who were helpful to you? In general, how did teachers respond to the new students?

RM: [Sighs] Well, they didn't make any difference between us that I can tell. Of course, I do remember that . . . nobody ever gave us any idea of how to get into the National Honor Society, what we had to do, or anything like that. Let's see, they had the National Honor Society. They had the student body council, student council, president, and all that kind of stuff. We didn't have any idea how to go about joining those. FHA [Future Homemakers of America], but we did get in home economics, but those extra clubs and stuff, nobody ever made us aware of what they were or how to get into them.

I: So as far as extracurricular activities, that first year you weren't involved. Was anyone involved in athletics at all?

RM: Oh, yes. There were some kids in football that first year, but I can't remember. Seemed like Bull Hayes . . . he was a big fellow. I can't remember if that was the first year, but there was always somebody going out for sports.

I: Did something like that help you make the transition, make black students any more accepted at Fayetteville High School than they might have been otherwise?

RM: No, no, no, because all that notoriety and stuff that Hayes got, he—when [the University] came up with scholarships, everybody got scholarships but him. Of course, he got one [from another college]. I don't know what kind he got offered, but nobody offered him anything around here where he would have been able to shine. I think he ended up going to—I can't remember where he went, but way out of state.

I: Coach Vandergriff was telling me something about him.

RM: Vandergriff, I think he was instrumental in getting some blacks [on the team] as I remember. And Benny Winborn. I don't know if they encouraged them or how they got [them], but I know [they did]. And that kind of helped us get into sports. We'd go to football games and stuff. I was just as glad as anybody else, but that was about all. That was about the biggest joy that we got out of going to high school, you know; it was supposed to be the happiest years of life. I haven't been to a class reunion yet. I just don't get an urge to go. It's not something that you look forward to doing. Preston [Lackey] was wanting to know why not a single black that I know goes to one. I think Preston went to one.

I: And your class had one this year, I believe, the Fourth of July, or was that his class?

RM: I don't know. I don't know.

I: So you never did feel in that first year or maybe even throughout your—all the time you went to high school here, that you—you didn't really feel a part of the student body? Or did that come later? Did it change? Did it get better at the end of your junior year and senior year?

RM: Well, it got a little better.

I: Did anyone, did you get support from anyone in particular at this time? Were there people in the church or in the black or the white community in Fayetteville that actively took an interest in encouraging you at this time that you can recall?

RM: I can't remember a soul. I just can't remember a soul.

I: Did you have a sense or feeling when you were going to school in '54 that you were some kind of pioneer, that you were breaking down some barrier?

RM: Yes, yes.

I: Did you have some conception of that yourself?

RM: Yes, I did. You know, because, like I say, all the news coverage and stuff that we had that first day when we went to register. . . .

I: Did that affect, do you think, the way you—

RM: No.

I: Did you feel any more pressure, I guess is what I want to know, on yourself because of that?

RM: No, no. I'm from a Christian family, you know, church oriented, but I did remember one deacon though. His name was V. H. Utley. He gave us a lot of support.

I: This was from what church?

RM: St. James Baptist. He used to preach all the time, you know—learn all you can because, you know—the older people in the church, they used to preach, take advantage, learn, because they didn't have a chance. . . .

I: So when you say he gave you support, you mean he talked to you personally or just in a sermon would say something like that?

RM: Yes, yes, mostly [in a sermon]. He preached to us all the time. That was our family and another girl's family that went, that graduated with Preston. We all went to the same church. But that was the type of encouragement we got. You know, nobody prepared us any way. It was just something we had to do.

I: One of the things that we're interested in is trying to find out why things seemed to go so much more smoothly in Fayetteville than they did in other places in Arkansas and throughout the South. And some people think it may have been the influence of the University. Some think it was more a financial decision, that the board couldn't afford to pay to send these students to Fort Smith and Hot Springs. Or some think maybe that churches had something to do with it, or just the fact that there were not many black students, that there weren't enough to make whites feel very threatened. Do you think any of those are good possibilities or [was it] something else?

RM: I think a good possibility is that they had just built a new high school and suspect it was costing them too much money to send us away to school. That's what I think. That's what I've always thought.

I: So you see it as an economic thing as much as anything else.

RM: Yes, that's the way I see it.

I: Mrs. Morgan, do you think it would have made a difference if instead of seven black students, there had been seventy? Would that have made it a bigger deal, you think, in Fayetteville? In other words, the fact that there were so few blacks that the white community didn't really feel that you constituted any threat had something to do with it also?

RM: Yes. That's right.

I: Now, you had gone to Lincoln School for all your school career up to this time.

RM: Yes. And I'll tell you who did prepare us. I said nobody prepared us, but I fibbed. Miss Dawkins, the principal.

I: I've heard her name mentioned several times.

RM: Minnie B. Dawkins. She prepared us. She did the preparing. She was the one that prepared us. Yeah, she was the one that was instrumental in preparing us.

I: Everyone I talk to brings her name up; that she was very instrumental in making a smooth transition. Now, I talked to a lady who taught in the white elementary school, and she said even before integration there were some times—for instance, the white school would be having a program, and students from Lincoln would go over there. White students would go to Lincoln.

RM: 'Cause I know we used to go over to Leverett School when they were putting on an operetta.

I: So there'd been some contact, black and white, before the integration.

RM: We used to go to the University also. For, oh, plays and, well, let's see, what did we go and see? She took us to the University to see something. *Snow White*, I think. And what else did she do? We went to Washington School, different schools. And then she used to take us to Philander [Smith College], too, you know. We used to sing. And I remember every time we went, we got honorable mention. We got a little old thing—we did good. We did good for ninth graders, you know. She used to take us. She just used to expose us to different stuff. I guess to prepare us for transition. She just used to do that kind of stuff. You don't know how fortunate you were to have her until she's gone.

I: Prior to this time, thinking back, what is your impression of living in Fayetteville? Were you aware it was a pretty segregated community or was not a segregated community?

RM: Let's see. I can't remember. The human relations council was responsible for getting some segregation stopped.

I: Looking back on that now, do you have a different perspective on it than you did when you were going through it? I mean, sometimes when you're young and going through an experience, things don't sink in. Later, looking back, you look at it differently. How do you look at that time now?

RM: Well, I still think it's about the same. You know, I think students belong to a whole lot more things, but I'm not sure if they feel any better about belonging. As long as it's been integrated, it should be a lot more—something. I don't know. I don't think the kids really feel a part of it. Of course, they've got a black club. There's a black teacher over there, so they've got an organization mainly for black students, which is good because that helps you to adjust. We didn't have anything like that. So we didn't—only thing we felt comfortable about was joining the glee club. That's because the teacher wanted us to join. Most of us were in glee club and sang with the choir and all that kind of stuff. It was just something that we enjoyed doing. And that's, as far as I know, that's the only thing we joined. Glee club.

PRESTON LACKEY JR.

Preston Lackey Jr., born in Fort Smith but a longtime resident of Fayetteville, was, along with his sisters, Roberta and Elnora, among the original seven black students to enroll in Fayetteville High School in the fall of 1954.

INTERVIEWER: Mr. Lackey, what I'd like to do is start out with just your remembrances of the situation that existed in 1954 and how you recall what happened in those days when the high school was integrated.

PRESTON LACKEY JR.: OK. Originally, we went to school over here til the ninth grade at Lincoln School. And then after that, you either went to Fort Smith or wherever you wanted to go if your folks could afford to send you. And sometime along—probably, I don't know the exact year—they started paying for us to go to school. Well, when I got out of ninth grade, I went to Hot Springs. Some of the others went to Fort Smith. Then in '54, yes, '54, we were able to go here at Fayetteville High, and that was my first year. I was a junior at that time. I really didn't know whether I wanted to go or not. I wanted to go back to Hot Springs, but I didn't have the finances to go, so—

I: Let me ask you, how did that work? You went to Hot Springs for a year?

PL: Yes.

I: And that was your sophomore year.

PL: Yes.

I: How did that work as far as funding went, and how were arrangements made for you to stay, and things like that?

PL: Well, I think the school did all that. The school board or somebody did it. They paid the rent and for keep. I never did see any figures on it, but at the time there were two of us going to Hot

Springs, and I don't know really how many were going to Fort Smith; probably pretty close to a dozen, I imagine.

I: You stayed with—just with a family down there?

PL: Yes, we stayed with a family.

I: Now, who arranged [it]? Did you have to arrange that yourself?

PL: No, no, I don't think—not that I can recall.

I: You were assigned a family that you would stay with.

PL: Well—it's been so long I can't remember. Now, I stayed with —Bobby Morgan was going, he was going down to Hot Springs, and I went down there with him, and we stayed at the same place. And the year before that, Homer Smith went with him, and then Homer didn't go back. His folks got sick, so he went to work. And I went down there with him. I don't recall just how they did that, or who found the place or what.

I: But you didn't know these people before you went down there?

PL: I didn't know them, no.

I: Were they relatives of someone you know or . . . ?

PL: No. I'll tell you what might have been . . . Homer and Bobby played football for the school down there. The coach might have arranged it for them; I don't know. Because I think he was up here going to school at the time, and I think he might have influenced them to go down there. But anyway, like I say, I can't really recall. They had room, and I stayed there.

I: It was an all-black school in Hot Springs.

PL: Yes, Langston.

I: Langston.

PL: Yes, no longer there.

I: So, you'd gone to school at Lincoln School in Fayetteville through grades nine—

PL: Well, actually from about fourth through ninth. We just moved here—we lived out in Cane Hill up till then. We moved here in '47. . . . I went to school over here [Fayetteville] from, oh, I think it was fourth grade, third or fourth grade. I think I was fourth grade when I moved here. I went there to the ninth grade.

I: So your plans were to finish school then in Hot Springs, which you originally intended to do.

PL: Really, I did.

I: Do you remember when you first found out about the Supreme Court decision, *Brown,* and how it was going to affect things and how it was going to affect you?

PL: I barely kind of remember it. I was down there [Hot Springs] at the time, I believe, when that came through. But, like I say, I'd still kind of made plans to go back down there, but financially couldn't, so . . . I paid for just laundry and things like that mostly.

I: How about meals?

PL: They would provide our meals.

I: That was taken care of. No, room and board, that was taken care of.

PL: That was taken care of. I don't know whether, I don't know whether there was any tuition. More than likely there was. I don't know, since we didn't live there. I didn't mind it here so much after I got started, but I kind of dreaded to start it. I didn't know what I was going to run into because some of the other schools had a lot of problems. I'll never forget that day we went, that first day. Well, we'd gone over before for—oh, I think we went over, oh, can't think what you call it now.

I: Sort of an orientation kind of deal?

PL: Yes, yes. But I think when we went over, there was some confusion about the time, and we were the only ones there. I think it was Peggy and myself, Peggy Taylor. We were juniors. We were in the same class. We were among two in the class. And we got there late or something—something, or a different day or something—and met with Miss Karnes. She was our homeroom teacher. She was a lot of help. Bernice Karnes, I believe. . . . She helped us. But anyway, the day—the first day we went, my dad took us, and we really didn't know what to expect. Lot of the other schools had had a lot of problems, you know. Things went on outside as you go to school. But we got there. . . . It was myself and Peggy and my cousin Virginia Smith Denton, or sister Elnora, at the time, and my sister Roberta and Mary Mae Blackburn. We didn't see a bunch of people standing around. Just like you'd go to school every day. We was kind of relieved there wasn't a lot of confusion going on.

I: Do you remember what the first day was like once you got to the school?

PL: Well, I remember a little of it. We went to—it was pretty close to the time for school to take up or time to be in your homeroom. We went right to our homeroom. We went in and took a seat. And a couple of fellows introduced themselves—Jerry Riggins, Parker Rushing; I remember them. And probably Dixie Jackson. They all introduced themselves. It kind of got off to a pretty good start. It's been so long, it's hard to remember exactly.

I: Now, that first year there were two of you in the junior class, is that right?

PL: Two in the junior class. Let's see—two in the junior class, and, let's see, I had two sisters and a cousin. I think there were four or five in the sophomore class. I can't remember—Kenneth Morgan came in there some time, but I can't recall exactly when he came in. . . . Because his folks had moved to California. He came in there sometime. He didn't go very long because he—I think he wound up going in the military shortly.

I: But you had two sisters who were sophomores?

PL: Yes, and I had a cousin, another young lady, Mary, Mary Blackburn.

I: Do you remember any times of . . . any unusual tension or trouble there other than what would normally be expected?

PL: No, the normal thing.

I: What did you find the student body to be, the white students—generally accepting or standoffish?

PL: Well, yes, pretty accepting. Of course, there were a few who were kind of standoffish. I've always been able to get around stuff like that.

I: You never encountered much harassment of any kind?

PL: No, not really. I didn't. I think, I think my sisters probably—I was telling her yesterday and, you know, . . . she had a little—not big problems, but maybe words, you know, . . . I only recall one incidence, really. At the time, I didn't think anything about it. We were going to class, and I'd gotten confused and gotten in the wrong seat. And this one guy, he said something about Sambo, you know. . . . I'd kind of forgot until I got to thinking about it yesterday. . . . That's about the only thing I ever really recall that anybody said to me.

I: Were any of the black students in that year '54 involved in athletics, band, anything like that, extracurricular activities?

PL: Yes, I think some were in the chorus, probably, and some of these other clubs. I assume my sister was in something; I don't remember exactly—one of the clubs, I think. I was in something. I've got a yearbook—I've got a '56, but my '55, I don't know what happened to it. Student council, what I'm trying to say. I was in it for—I guess the first year I was there, I guess. Because I looked in '56, and I didn't see it in '56.

I: Now, was that an appointed thing or elective, or how did that work?

PL: Yes, I believe, yeah—it was elective.

I: Elective?

PL: Yes.

I: That's rather remarkable, it seems to me.

PL: Yeah, well, I think how we did it is—I don't know how many rooms consisted of the junior class at that time, but I think each homeroom [had a representative]. I think that's the way they did it. Each junior homeroom. And I happened to be [the representative] for our homeroom. Well, I think, the president or some of the other officers were in my room also. I kind of enjoyed that. I was in the student council for one year.

I: How did the year you were here, the first year you were here, compare with your experience in Hot Springs? How would you compare the two?

PL: [Laughs] I'd say they were just about, pretty much similar. Yes . . . I was going with people I really didn't know, and I got to know them in Hot Springs. Of course, when I went to the first year, I didn't know anybody there but one fellow either, so—yes, it was pretty similar. It was pretty similar I'd say.

I: One thing we've been trying to determine is—you've already mentioned this—is that in several places in Arkansas and throughout the South there was widespread resistance to integration.

PL: Yes, yes. Like I say, that first day, I didn't know what to look for. But I was so relieved that I didn't see a bunch of people standing on the sidewalk and shouting. I had seen that on TV from other places.

I: Mr. Lackey, why do you think that didn't happen in Fayetteville?

PL: I don't know. I think basically the people of Fayetteville were a lot calmer about stuff like that, I believe. 'Cause I had been in places like Fort Smith. You can tell, it's just fifty miles south. But it seemed like in this area the blacks and the whites always got along pretty good. Of course, at that time, I remember, you didn't go into restaurants and eat, but you could go there and get food and leave and stuff like that. A lot of places you couldn't do that.

I: It is my understanding that even Springdale was almost without blacks.

PL: They didn't have any. There may have been a few. Rogers didn't have any. But I think Rogers has a very few, and most of them are people that are coming and working for companies.

I: One of the things we're trying to discover is what it was about

Fayetteville that made it different from Fort Smith, which as you say is not that far away, or Springdale.

PL: Yes, there are still problems down there. I used to go to Fort Smith a lot, but mostly I was in the black community when I went down there.

I: Several people I talked to said they thought perhaps it was the presence of the University.

PL: Well, that could have something to do with it because there was a black student [Silas Hunt] to enroll in about 1948—

I: I believe that's right. I think it was in the law school.

PL: Yeah, I knew him. I can't think of his name right now. . . . But he, he came over, well, like I say, there used to be a playground. He would come over, some of those guys going to the University, they'd come over and play basketball over here. But I think that helped. I think that helped somewhat. We just got along a little better in this part of the country.

I: How important do you think it was, or do you think it was important at all, that there were only a few black students entering the schools? There were six or seven, you said.

PL: I think there were six. I remember—there started out six, I think.

I: How significant do you think that was? There weren't that many black students entering at the time. Would there have been a difference if there were seventy, in other words?

PL: Probably, probably. I think it might. White people didn't seem to feel threatened by it.

I: One thing that struck me is the sort of matter-of-fact way in which integration took place.

PL: Sure.

I: I guess one of the things we're trying to get at is why it was different here.

PL: Yes. Well, you know, that [Fayetteville High School] was a pretty new school. Seemed like they built that in '51 or '52. And I've often wondered if they thought, you know, it wouldn't be better to use that money on the school than to send people off to another—

I: I've heard that mentioned also. Financial reasons may have entered into it because it was obviously going to be very expensive.

PL: Sure, I mean, I'd say there were probably twelve to fourteen people they were sending off. That doesn't sound like a lot, but financially it could be.

I: You finished up at—

PL: Finished at Fayetteville High. I went two years. I went '54–'55 season and got out in '56.

I: You talked about the community when you lived here back in the fifties and the fact that you were aware that it was a segregated society to some extent in terms of restaurants and public places.

PL: Yes, but nobody bothered you. I guess it was just unwritten law, you know. I don't guess you'd call it a law, but that's the way it was.

I: Did you start to see a change in that at all after the schools had been integrated?

PL: Yes, sometime after, yes. The only sign I ever saw in Fayetteville that said "Colored Side" was at Harmon playfield [at Fayetteville High School]. They had a sign down there that said "For Colored." Well, shortly after we started going to school there, it disappeared.

I: You were very much more aware of segregation in Fort Smith, on the whole, than you were in Fayetteville.

PL: Yes, right.

I: Did you get any support or encouragement from any other group or person or segment—church, individuals, white or black— in this town?

PL: No, not that I can recall. I don't think. If you wanted to go to school, you went. If you didn't—well, our folks wanted us to go to school. That's [why] we moved to Fayetteville. The little school we went to down—we lived at Cane Hill of all places, you might get to go every three months or six months if they had the money, but usually it was like three or four months. More black schooling here, so we moved here. I guess—well, all of us got through school one way or the other. Some of them went to college. Some of my brothers and sisters did. About three of them finished college.

I: Let me go back to earlier. Do you recall anything at all about when you first found out that school was going to be integrated here and that you'd be one of the first blacks—

PL: I was going to school in Hot Springs when they came out with this—some of us, we discussed it. I said, well, I want to come back, but I don't know. I'll try to come back. But I really don't recall a lot about how I felt about it, you know.

I: You also then, I guess, were one of the first, *the* first class to graduate, black student to graduate from Fayetteville High School.

PL: Yes, yes I was.

I: Did that occasion any kind of stir at all, do you remember?

PL: I don't recall that it did. I never thought much about it. In high school, when you finish high school, you just want to get out. I guess maybe I was—I was pretty excited. I was pretty excited about graduation. Long way to have to walk across before we'd get that diploma.

I: So that was, what, '56?

PL: '56, yes, yes.

I: There were two black students in that class?

PL: Yes.

I: Peggy Taylor and yourself.

PL: Yes.

I: What you have told me is pretty much in line with what everyone else told me. It just wasn't the big issue here that it was a lot of places.

PL: No, no.

I: In terms of protest and people making a big cause out of it.

PL: I never did hear of any protests. I didn't hear of any. So that helps.

I: Sure it does. I'm sure it does. Do you remember at the time, Mr. Lackey, being conscious at all of the significance that was attached to it? Did you have any sense that you were sort of a trailblazer?

PL: No, I never thought about that, I sure didn't.

I: You didn't feel any additional pressure?

PL: No, I don't think I did. I don't believe I did. I enjoyed it. I got to know a lot of people. Some of them I still see. They remember me if I don't remember them.

I: In terms of the faculty, administration, did you find them, in general, helpful, willing to help you?

PL: Yes. I remember Mrs. Ellis, Mrs. G. C. Ellis was awfully helpful. All of them were that I had. That was another thing. I was trying to remember who all my teachers were . . . I remember Mrs. Ellis and Mrs. [Mary] Heflin. Miss Karnes was very helpful.

I: Before we conclude, is there anything else that I haven't addressed that sticks out in your memory about those days, looking back on it now?

PL: Miss [Minnie] Dawkins was an awful lot of help. She was a teacher and a principal over here at Lincoln School at that time. I don't know where you'd get hold of her. She's still living. . . .

I: Apparently, there was some degree of linkage between [the] black and white communities and the elementary schools even before integration. I've had teachers tell me that when they had a program, they would go over to the black school, and the black children would come over to their schools.

PL: Oh, yes.

I: So apparently there was some foundation laid there.

PL: Yes, we used to go to Jefferson quite a bit, go see a play.

I: Do you think that had anything to do with the ease with which it came off later?

PL: Could be.

I: Those things are hard to assess. It's hard to say what made a difference.

PL: Yes.

I: It was definitely different than it was in some of the other places in the state, and one of the things we're trying to do is get a handle on it.

PL: I was trying to remember some of those places that were having all the problems.

I: Of course, Sheridan—Sheridan voted to integrate the same time Fayetteville did, but there was so much opposition that they, the school board, a day later rescinded it. But Fayetteville made the news I recall.

PL: I don't ever remember seeing it in the paper. At the time, you see, I was away from home when it first came out. Here's a picture. Yeah, that's my sisters. Now, they had a picture of my sisters and— they had the girls' picture in *Jet*. I don't remember seeing it. I don't know where I was at the time they took the picture. I was going to school at that time, but they had them in *Jet* and a little write-up.

I: Back in '54, you think?

PL: Yeah, it was '54 or '55.

I: Well, I'll be.

PL: You know, I believe that's the only time I recall any writing on it.

N. GLENN SOWDER

N. Glenn Sowder, a native of Fayetteville, was a student at Fayetteville High School in 1954 when the school was integrated. His mother was for many years a teacher in the Fayetteville Public School System. Mr. Sowder currently resides in Fayetteville.

INTERVIEWER: First of all, I want to ask you what you remember about how you found out about the decision to integrate the schools?

N. GLENN SOWDER: I believe that I probably read about it in the paper during my sophomore year in high school, which would have been late 1953 or early 1954.

I: So, you were a sophomore.

GS: Yes, I was a sophomore in high school.

I: That's the tenth grade, which is the first year that you attend the high school.

GS: Fayetteville changed: it had a ninth through twelfth high school until 1952. Then in '52 it became a three-year high school in a new building and a three-year junior high in the old high school building. And I went to the junior high only one year; I had attended Washington Elementary one through eight. So, there were a lot of changes going on at the high school at that time.

I: I just read about the fact that they built a new school.

GS: And it was called the new high school, and is still called that by most of us. To those of us who attended the original high school, the present building is still the "new" high school forty years later. Of course, the old one is gone, unfortunately. It was a beautiful building, and it would have been nice to have preserved it.

I: Do you remember the first day of school? Anything that was unusual?

GS: There was discussion during the spring as to whether or not there would be any black athletes. Black athletes already had a reputation—Jackie Robinson had come a long time before that in 1946 or '47. He had broken the color line in professional baseball. There was a discussion about whether we would have any good athletes who would help our team in the fall of '54 when the black students came to school with us. However, there were none. Preston Lackey and Peggy Taylor were the only two students who came to Fayetteville High that year. Two black students, and neither one of them were athletes. So, really it didn't have any impact on us in our junior year at all.

I: So, you were on the team?

GS: I tried to play. I did play football, basketball, and track while I was in high school. These were the only sports offered at that time at Fayetteville High for boys or girls. Integration had virtually no impact, and I honestly don't recall anyone making any disparaging or negative remarks about the prospect of having black students in the school with us. I remember no incident of anyone having made any untoward remarks to Peggy or Preston. They seemed readily accepted by the faculty and student body.

I: Did you have classes with them?

GS: Yes, I did have. I had at least two or three classes with each of them.

I: Did you feel like they were treated the same as other students?

GS: Yes, I did. It was very pleasant and very positive, and as I look back, I am very proud. The reality is that integration in the Fayetteville school system was a considerably different situation than in Little Rock public schools, or in Helena, where the percentage might have been fifty-fifty, black students to white students, or even seventy to eighty percent black. The percentage of black students in Fayetteville was very, very low. Numerically, it was not a problem with us. The individuals we were dealing with were extremely good citizens. I don't remember Peggy or Preston ever getting in trouble or doing anything out of line. In fact, they were better citizens than a lot of the white students. That certainly can't be said of a lot of us at Fayetteville High.

A very colorful and popular person in those years was a black man named Buddy Hayes. Buddy had the shoeshine stand at the Dickson Street Barber Shop, and it was rumored at one time or another that Buddy made book on sporting events. He also had a band in which he played the trumpet. Buddy and his band played for most of the high school dances. Then, there weren't as many bands available as there are now. He had white members in his band as well as other black members. Furthermore, Buddy was the unofficial mayor of the black community at that time and well accepted by blacks and whites alike. Of course, there were opprobrious appellations other than "the black community," which were common at that time. I had trouble with my father, though my dad was truly a good Christian man. He used the word "nigger" and the word "colored." He also used the word "darky," and referred to the part of town east of the courthouse where the black community primarily, or entirely, lived as "Tin Cup" or "Nigger Holler." I never heard these terms used at school. Other adults outside of school would occasionally say them. Later, I had trouble with my dad from time to time when he would slip and say those words before my children. I had to say, "Hey, Dad, you are going to get my children in trouble if you say things like that in front of them, and they go to school and repeat them."

Buddy was in fact the leader in the black community and the spokesman for it. I would go down to the barber shop and visit him. In fact, if you went to get a haircut, you would always visit with him. He was a real football fan. In fact, at that time, black citizens were not allowed to sit in the stands at the University football games. They would go in at the south gate and sit in folding chairs at the corner of the end zone. There would be twenty or thirty. Buddy would come to Fayetteville High School games. He was a good community leader and a fan. I remember one day, a few years later, when Little Rock Central was having its integration problems and Buddy was financially well off, secure, and had a new Mercury sedan. I said, "Hey, Buddy, why don't we go to Little Rock and show those people how people are supposed to act. You ride in the back seat and I'll drive." And he said, "Sowder, you are dumber than I thought you were, you will get us both killed." He understood how the world really was and not just in Fayetteville. He was a leader and a moderating force in the black community.

The first year of integration was totally uneventful in Fayetteville. And then questions started being asked the next year because we had significantly more black students with the start of the 1955–56 school year.

I: And that year there were some athletes?

GS: Yes, there were some athletes. Bull Hayes, William "Bull" Hayes, turned out to be the most famous. He should have made all-state; I think he only made all-district. But he went to the University of Nebraska on a scholarship, and then ended up playing at Joplin Junior College one year, and then played his final two years at Arkansas AM&N, which is now University of Arkansas at Pine Bluff. Bull didn't start a game or play much at all as a sophomore at FHS. Bull was a fullback. There was another small running back named Ralph Hayes, and then there was a tall, skinny kid named James Funkhouser. I believe that Bobby Morgan also came out for the football team that year. Bull was the only one that ended up being an outstanding player and a star for the varsity two years later. The others either dropped out of athletics or may have moved to another town, I don't know. In 1955–56, Harry Vandergriff was our coach, Mrs. Bunn Bell our principal, and Wayne White the superintendent; I think they handled it masterfully. I barely remember one meeting that took less than five minutes when Coach Vandergriff told us that Russellville, Harrison, and Fort Smith, Arkansas, wouldn't play us if our black players dressed out and/or played. I recall no discussion among the players at all. We just said, "Hey, if they aren't going to play us with them [the black athletes], then we aren't going to play them." We actually had eight games that year instead of the ten that high schools usually have. I remember we added one game because three canceled. We picked somebody else up; I am not sure who it was. As a result of this, the attitude that other Arkansas high schools had, especially in the southern part of the state, was that Fayetteville had to play in the Ozark Conference, which included Joplin High School, Springfield Central, and Springfield Parkview. We had been playing Springfield Central all along, and then they added a second high school, Parkview, but we didn't play them my senior year. I don't know who we added; maybe it was Huntsville or Siloam Springs. We had planned not to play Huntsville, but we probably added them back whenever we were short games on our schedule.

Also, I think Rogers, Springdale, and Siloam, since they had no black community or a limited black community, deserve credit, too, in that they went ahead and played us, and didn't force us to play all Missouri schools for the next few years. There were a lot of people who had a positive hand in all of this. I don't remember one of the teams that we played against making any derogatory remarks or any

profane or racial slurs. Of course, Bull, Ralph, and James seldom
got into varsity games in 1955. They played junior varsity or B team
games. There were never any issues since there were no occasions
for such. I don't remember any townspeople trying to rabble-rouse
at all.

During my senior year, Ralph Hayes, a natural athlete, was on the
team. He was a small man, but very well built, with a lot of muscle
definition and athletic ability. I can remember his crawling the
ropes in gym class and how his biceps would just bulge and bounce
up and down. He was a well-adjusted, normal human being, well
accepted by all the students. He would flirt with the white girls as
well as with the black, and though there was a touch of tension over
that, there was also tension among the white guys who flirted with
white girls as well. It was more of a sexual than a racial issue—of
who was giving whom attention, that sort of thing—rather than a
black-and-white issue. I never felt it was racially motivated tension—
just normal adolescent reaction between the boys and girls.

I: What do you remember about the community, about how the
blacks were accepted in the community?

GS: I grew up in the First Baptist Church, and I remember that I
was very much aware that our church sponsored foreign missionar-
ies. We would spend our church money to send one of our church
members to Africa to be a missionary to provide medical care and
to preach the gospel of Jesus Christ, but we didn't let black people
attend our church. They had to have a separate church, which was
about four blocks away, and I was never really comfortable with
that concept of "separate but equal." In fact, I was shocked when in
junior high, my dad took me to Little Rock to the state capitol, and
I asked, "Why do they have two drinking fountains?" and "What
does 'colored' mean on the drinking fountain?" There just hadn't
been that much difference in my mind. When I was a little boy, I
had gone to play with Vincent Lesh up on Mount Sequoyah at his
house, which was within a block or two of Tin Cup. We would play
with black kids, play ball and that sort of thing, and it was memo-
rable because I hadn't played with black children before. It didn't
take ten minutes to figure out that they played ball just like I did;
the difference was that they didn't have the socioeconomic advantage that I did. They lived in rather poor houses because they
worked at the laboring end of the economic structure. Not that I
was well off: my dad was a postal clerk, and my mom was a school

teacher. By comparison, however, I was significantly well off. But we played the same games and liked the same things.

I never heard a community leader or dissident say, "Don't do it, keep them down, keep them out." Of course, we had to live with Governor Orval Faubus's decision to use the National Guard to keep black people from entering Little Rock High School. The reality is that Little Rock's superintendent of schools in 1957 was Virgil Blossom, who had been the superintendent of the schools in Fayetteville. He had actually been a football coach, a principal, then became Fayetteville's superintendent of schools. He had been hired about the time that I was in the eighth grade as superintendent of the Little Rock school system, and he was the one who said that we are going to abide by the federal law, and we are going to integrate Little Rock Central High School. Then Faubus came up against him. By that time, I had joined the Arkansas National Guard in 1955 between my junior and senior years in high school. I was at Coffeyville Junior College in Coffeyville, Kansas, playing football in 1957 when I was federalized with the Arkansas National Guard because I still belonged to the Headquarters, Battery 936 Field Artillery Battalion in Fayetteville. However, because we never had to send the whole unit to Little Rock, members of the guard who were students were allowed to stay in school. A few members of my unit volunteered and did go to Little Rock. They let us go to school with the provision that we would come back on the weekends, and we actually got paid for twenty-nine days of active duty.

I: So, you almost had to go to Little Rock?

GS: I could have gone to Little Rock, and some of the people did, and some entire units were sent. It was very interesting. The 101st Airborne Division was on one side of the fence of the ballpark and the Arkansas National Guard was on the other side of the fence. And I remember the story being told to me that the 101st Airborne, which was active federal troops, were there to keep the Arkansas National Guard from going to the high school and restricting entrance of the black students. It was a very emotional thing. And then President [Dwight] Eisenhower federalized the Arkansas National Guard, which is why I went on active duty. When Faubus just called certain units of the National Guard to keep the black students from going, that didn't affect us at all, because they only needed one hundred National Guardsmen standing in front of the doors. But to make sure that Faubus didn't have any troops that he could command, President Eisenhower federalized the entire Arkansas National Guard. . . .

An interesting sidelight to that was that when you go on active duty, the military always gives you a physical so they can determine the liability for service-related injuries when you get out. So, one weekend while we were federalized, they took the Fayetteville unit to Fort Chaffee to give us physical and dental exams. . . . In the dental clinic that day, there were about six people giving dental exams, and only one was black. The people that were in the dental clinic were not necessarily from Arkansas and probably weren't from Arkansas. They had the one black dental technician do the x-rays on all the white Arkansas guardsmen's teeth. So there was a black man sticking his fingers in all of those "bubbas'" mouths. There was some spitting and some comments about that. I don't know of any-one who bit him or refused to have their teeth x-rayed, and many of us had a good laugh.

ɪ: Why do you think the integration went so smoothly here?

ɢꜱ: For one reason, Virgil Blossom had paved the way for inte-gration while superintendent of schools in Fayetteville before he moved to Little Rock. And for the reason that Fayetteville is such a diverse community, and the liberal influence of the University. And a lot of it had to do with there being only three-hundred-some-plus black people in a twenty thousand person town. In 1948 the first black student [Silas Hunt] entered the U of A law school on a vol-untary basis. Though there was some discussion about opening the campus to black students, I do not recall any real challenge or a law-suit. The time was right for change, and a good student came along and said, "Hey, I am willing to face the challenge of being your first black student and breaking the ice for future generations," and inte-gration went ahead and happened. But there were very few, if any, blacks at the University of Arkansas when I went there; I entered the fall of '56, and on that freshman football team I had teammates who said that, even when they were seniors, if they brought in black ath-letes, they wouldn't stay. These were people—such as a kid who became a doctor from Wilson, Arkansas. And I had a friend from Memphis who felt the same way. They just felt very strongly that the races needed to be totally separate but equal; of course that was a euphemism. There was also strong support for integration in other parts of the state that I became aware of when I returned to the University two years later, at least among the student population.

I: Were you born in Fayetteville?

GS: I was born here. My mother's dad moved his family here in 1919. In 1921 he bought some land between North and Adams and Gregg and the railroad tracks, about four acres. . . . I am a third-generation Fayetteville resident. My mom moved here when she was six years old, my dad when he was about a year old, and they lived the remainder of their lives here. With the exception of the time I spent in the army and a couple of years I moved around after that, I have been a Fayetteville resident.

As a sidelight, while I was playing football in the army and stationed in Fort Hood in 1965, our football team played Arkansas AM&N from Pine Bluff. I got to play against Bull Hayes again. He was a senior fullback on that team when I was playing in the army. . . .

As far as integration goes . . . I had a tryout with the Denver Broncos and played three exhibition games with them. On a road trip to Fort Worth, Texas, to play against the Dallas Texans, our black athletes found out at the last minute that the hotel the Broncos were staying at would not give them rooms. They had to be bused across town to a black hotel, and it visibly bothered and shook them up. That was another part of my education in discrimination. That Fort Worth was still a segregated city, at least there were not any city laws or ordinances to protect the black athletes in 1961, was a shock to me.

It was a different world, and at that time black people did not spend the night in Springdale or Rogers, Arkansas, or Monet, Missouri.

JOHN LEWIS

John Lewis, a Fayetteville banker and civic leader, was a student at the city's high school during the years of its integration.

INTERVIEWER: Do you remember how you found out about the decision to integrate the high school?

JOHN LEWIS: No, not specifically, I don't.

I: Do you remember the first day of school that year?

JL: No, I remember the summer leading up to that year, and there was a lot of friendship between the various classes and so forth, and we had a lot of group activities, such as camping and picnics, and church activities, and there was a lot of communication back and forth between the various classes. My last year in junior high was at Hillcrest, and when we graduated from Hillcrest, we went over to the Fayetteville High School building. And my class was a pretty cohesive class; we were a real athletic group; we were undefeated in football, and then we won the state championship in basketball.

I: So, do you remember hearing about the decision to integrate the schools that summer at all?

JL: Yes, I think that is when it became commonly known in the group that it was going to be integrated. It really wasn't that big of a deal. I lived on Washington Street, which is not far from "Tin Cup" [area in Fayetteville where blacks lived], and I had worked at the Ford Company and had a number of older black friends, people that I knew and that I had known and been friendly with all my life. So, it wasn't any particular big deal as far as I was concerned.

I: Were there any black students in your class?

JL: Yes, my remembrance of it is that there was somewhere between five to nine—seven comes to mind, but I am not really sure about that.

I: Then you were on the football team, right?

JL: And the basketball team.

I: There were some black students on the football team.

JL: Yes, I don't think very many. My recollection is that there were just very few, and they had not had any prior playing experience, and the ones that we had didn't start; they weren't the stars of the team, but they were definitely part of the team and had equal opportunity. And they had equal opportunity bècause Harry Vandergriff was the coach, and he made sure that everybody had an equal chance to do the best that they could.

I: Do you remember the problems that occurred about the teams who wouldn't play you if you brought your black players?

JL: Yes, I sure do. We voted as a team, and we had a real good football team that year. A number of the players went on to play at the University and one in particular went on to the pros. And we really had quite a good team that year that I was a sophomore in high school. We just voted not to play the teams that didn't want our whole team to come down and play them.

I: Do you feel that this was an easy decision for the team?

JL: Yes, it was an easy decision as I remember. I don't remember even having any discussions about it. As I remember, the discussion, or how we found out about it, we were sitting in the stands at Harmon playfield, and Vandergriff—I can't remember the teams—I think it was Russellville and I am not sure who else, but he just said that they would let us bring only our white players, but we couldn't bring our blacks, and so we just voted not to play.

I: Were the black players at this meeting?

JL: Yes, they were there. But it didn't matter. They were accepted as a part of the community and as a part of the team. It involved the community background and the times that we were living in back in the early fifties—times of optimism and great promise for the country, and people firmly believed that everyone had an equal opportunity and that the Constitution ruled and that we really shouldn't discriminate, and everybody ought to have an equal chance, at least that was the way it was felt in Fayetteville. Integration wasn't anything in particular new to the community, because the University had been integrated several years prior to that without any difficulty.

I: Do you remember any incidents between black students and white students at all?

JL: No, I don't remember a single one. I considered most of the

black students friends of mine; I would take them home after
school. I had an old car then, and none of them did. They didn't
have any transportation, and they all walked, and we lived probably
within four or five blocks of one another back more toward the east
part of town, and the high school was toward the west part of town,
so they rode with me back and forth, and a number of other people
had cars too, and it just didn't seem like it was fair to get out of
school and get in a car and drive home while the blacks walked. Or
get out of football practice near dark and we have a car to get home
and they had to walk home. So, we generally just—everybody just
kind of piled in and we gave them a ride home.

I: And I heard they used to pile in your car at lunchtime, too.

JL: Yes, we did that, too. And other people's, you know, it was—
my particular class got along better with black students than others
because the leadership of my group came out of the Methodist and
Episcopal and Presbyterian and Christian churches, and that had
been discussed in church meetings and so forth—

I: Integration had been discussed?

JL: Yes, integration, and what was going to happen, and then I
think that the atmosphere of the school was very important, due to
the leadership. Louise Bell, who was the principal, was the established leader of the school and a great disciplinarian, and someone
who believed in treating humans properly, and right, and fairly; and
Harry Vandergriff, a war hero and a very handsome, powerful individual who just would not tolerate any misbehavior or racism, or
anything like that. So, I think that the atmosphere of the school had
an enormous impact on the success of the integration. Even today, I
can't conceive of Mrs. Bell or Coach Vandergriff allowing anyone or
any group to create any problems in the school. They just wouldn't
tolerate it.

I: Tell me a little bit more about the church support.

JL: I don't remember a great deal about it. I just remember that
not only the churches but also the leadership organizations in the
school had a preparation time for people to understand that something different in the South was happening and that we were going
to make it successful here, and we weren't going to have any problems with it. We were led to understand that there was a difference
between equality and what was commonly termed then "equal-but-
separate" facilities; you know that was the kind of legal terminology
that had made segregation a way of life. We will give blacks equal

education in separate facilities; well, anybody with any curiosity and a right mind could go down and visit the black school [Lincoln School] and see that there wasn't any equal opportunity in the black school. Black students even had to leave town once they got to high school. Lincoln School was not an equal facility—it may have had good teachers, but it wasn't a school facility equal to that which the white kids were going to. So, even though we had good leadership as far as the churches and the school administration, anybody, any of the students with good sense, knew that there wasn't anything honest about the separate-but-equal facilities doctrine.

I: Why do you think that it went so smoothly here as opposed to Little Rock and other places?

JL: I think that it had to start with the leadership of the community, number one, and the culture of Fayetteville, which is a culture of education going back to how Fayetteville was settled. It was settled after the Indian treaty with the Cherokees of 1828 by people who emigrated across the mountains from Kentucky, Tennessee, and Virginia, and they were principally of British stock and had a very high regard for education, and there was a college in Fayetteville in 1840. Then in the 1860s during the Civil War, the community was pretty well devastated; the Confederates lost the battle and burned the square down and burned everything and scorched the earth as they retreated from Fayetteville so that the Yankees would not get any benefit from the victory in that battle. That happened in 1863 or '64, and yet in 1871 when the land-grant college was to be awarded to a community in an area in the state of Arkansas, this area, though it had less population and had been totally devastated by the Civil War, raised more money to put the land-grant college in Fayetteville than any other area in the state, and so that's a testimony to the culture of education that's been in this community for over 150 years. So, I think that the leadership of the community understood that we had this culture of education within the community; the average education was probably substantially higher in Washington County than in any other county or area within the state.

Because in 1954 Fayetteville was a small town and had strong leaders, the leaders believed that they ought to enforce the law of the land. When the Supreme Court decision came down, I think the decision was made to integrate immediately, and the leaders made sure that the decision was made and was carried forward. So I think, number one, that the community has a good educational background and its leaders probably possessed a little bit more liberal understanding of human relations; and, number two, I think we have a pretty unique leadership within the schools themselves to enforce the decision reached by the school board and the leadership of the community and the leaders within the schools; I think this is real important. Foresight and commitment established a system whereby on the first day of school, unfortunate incidents just didn't occur; they were choreographed, so to speak, so that all the leadership, student council, 26 Club, and all the clubs had a previous knowledge of what was taking place and how they were to act. So, you had great leadership and a system that worked—a system that was established by the leaders in the schools, and I am principally thinking of Louise Bell, and a very experienced teaching staff that was present at the high school, and the football and basketball coaches, Harry Vandergriff and Benny Winborn. They just didn't allow any misbehavior of any type. We had a lot of fun while we were in school; yet it was a very organized system that we went through; we did have a lot of fun, but did things differently. We enjoyed school, but at the same time there wasn't a lot of misbehavior or any misbehavior in the school; everybody knew where all the lines were, and I give Mrs. Bell the credit for having the foresight to establish a system where everybody knew what their role was in the system and what they could get away with.

I: What did you mean by the clubs having previous knowledge of the decision?

JL: The leadership clubs that were established in the high school, the student council principally being one, had retreats during the summers, and all of the officers and the people in those clubs—I was involved in a number of those clubs—went down to Mount Magazine with the teacher representative of each club present, and the students were allowed to participate in each organization's goal setting and were educated about what the particular function of that club or association was. So we had a number of clubs that you could call the leadership clubs, people who wanted to learn to become leaders or exert some leadership or desired to influence events within the school, had become members of or ran for student council or for colors or for different organizations. And a teacher was assigned to be the teacher-leader or sponsor of those clubs, and we would have retreats in the summer, and we would go

off and establish the goals and have good communication and for-
mulate the plan for reaching those goals.

We also had a very organized homeroom system where every
morning you came to a homeroom and had a period of homeroom
that was designed to create spirit within the schools because we had
contests; I can't remember them specifically, but I remember that
each homeroom had an *esprit de corps* of its own. . . . Everybody was
interested in seeing their homeroom be better, no matter what event
it was, whether it was intramural sports or building floats or whatever the activity might be, and the homeroom teachers were much
involved. My homeroom teacher was Mrs. G. C. Ellis; she was a history teacher, and she had a pretty profound impact on my life, even
though I only had one class under her. It was American Government, but she was a very outstanding teacher and very interested in
the development of students, as were most of the teachers of that
time. In fact, I think probably without question, all of the teachers
were interested in the development of young people, and they were
a very experienced older group. Although I wouldn't tell that to
their face right now, the ones who are still alive. But they had been
around a long time, had seen a lot. I have seen pictures of the high
school teachers in the thirties and forties, and we still had a lot of
those teachers in the mid-fifties.

You asked a question earlier about the athletics. Another problem we had was whenever we went to another city to play a team,
none of the restaurants would allow us to eat there, so we would
always take box lunches or dinners with us. At basketball, we played
all over the area. Football, we finally ended up having to play a lot of
Missouri teams because they were integrated and didn't mind playing us, but as I recall, we still took box lunches up there. No one
complained; it was just a fact of life.

I: Were there any blacks on student council?

JL: I honestly don't remember.

I: How did you get on student council and other clubs? Was it
elections?

JL: Student council—I think you were elected, schoolwide. My
thought is that the blacks were pretty well represented in all areas. I
don't really remember about the student council. It wouldn't have
been a big deal. The atmosphere of the school was to let black students seek their own level that they felt comfortable doing. If they
wanted to be in a particular club, there was nothing barring them.

I: You feel like the white students were accepting and supportive of them being in these clubs?

JL: Absolutely. I think 100 percent. The friends that I had accepted integration 100 percent without any reservation. Our thought was that we studied about the Civil War with all the problems, all the lynchings and the Ku Klux Klan, and knew about the injustice that had been done to the black people. And we knew that they didn't have equal opportunity even though prior to 1954 the law of the land said that they did have an equal opportunity, but anybody with any sense knew they did not. And we felt like it was only fair that they receive an equal opportunity to do whatever it was they wanted to do or accomplish. There were others in the school that weren't particularly friends of mine that weren't as enthusiastic about integration or didn't have that same feeling, but I don't remember any difficulties or any incidents or things like that. Disturbances caused by a white boy and a colored boy running into each other in the halls—but there was none of that. Disputes on the football field or at practice happen a lot of times, but I don't remember any.

I: You were the instigator of telling this whole story about integrating the Fayetteville schools. Why did you think it was so important?

JL: I had an industrial prospect as a guest in town about a year ago. He wanted to see the arena which is the new basketball [Bud Walton] arena at the University because it had been a source of controversy and had been in the newspaper, so we went to visit it, and as an afterthought I drove up the hill by the high school and said that this was the first integrated school in the South, and he wanted to get out of the car and take a picture, and he was just kind of overwhelmed by it. And it came to me that it was a significant piece of Fayetteville's history, and most of the people that were leaders in making it happen probably were still alive, and now was the time to get the story down so others can learn from what happened. I think it is one of the strengths of our country that despite the KKK and racial bigotry, we, as a country, spend a lot less energy fighting racial and ethnic battles than any other country in the world. I think that one of the strengths we have is the ability to live together to some degree in peace and have common goals and common aspirations. I think that the basis of all this, living in harmony . . . is a direct result of education, public education, which I think, even though maligned now, is one of the greatest assets our country has.

Through our system of public education, everyone has an understanding of the history of our country and the constitution and the founding principles of our country. We have injustices, admittedly, but they are not so divisive, and we don't spend as much energy on them as other countries do.

JIM BOB WHEELER

Jim Bob Wheeler, a native of Fayetteville and a well-known business-man, was a high school student in the first years of integrated classes at Fayetteville High School. He was a member of the school's football squad and has vivid recollections of his black teammates.

INTERVIEWER: Do you remember how you found out about the decision to integrate the high school?

JIM BOB WHEELER: I just remember being in school and we had some classmates that were black. And then I heard that this was the first group of blacks that had gone to school here.

I: It was the first integrated school in the South, so it was an historical event. No one really knew that at the time.

JW: I guess it never dawned on me that it was a big deal. Of course, I was born and raised here, like a lot of us were. I just never had thought about it, I guess.

I: Did you have classes with any of the black students?

JW: I think so, I played football with [William] Bull Hayes. Of course, I was just crazy about him. Preston Lackey was one of our real good friends in school. I don't remember having a class with him, but he was one of my favorite people, just a super nice guy. And one of the girls, seems like I had a class with Roberta Lackey; I think I did.

I: Do you remember any incidents that happened between the black and white students?

JW: You mean a bad incident?

I: Or anything.

JW: No, I really don't. . . . Hey, we were just all there.

I: Do you remember that the first year that the blacks played on the football team that some of the regularly scheduled games were canceled because those teams wouldn't play against black students?

JW: I do remember that. . . .I do remember that. The only bad experience I ever had with a black was the fact that Joplin had a running back that just happened to be black, and he was tougher than a pine knot. He used to just wear us out. I remember that. He was tough. We didn't have any problems that I can remember. . . . I had a problem one time; my dad used to be real big on being an individual, to stand up for what you believe and don't go along with the crowd and all that stuff that we have all heard. And I remember one time, we were in the restaurant business, and we were serving dinner out at Lake Wedington. It was in the summertime, and we had a lot of summer students that were at the University that were out there. And one of them was really bad-mouthing the situation, really bad. And I made some comment, you know, just in passing, "Hey, you know that I play football with a couple of [black] guys and we are just crazy about them." And it made him furious. I remember that. He got extremely upset. Of course, at the time I was just in high school, and he let me know real quick that I needed to keep my opinions to myself. My dad, I talked to my dad about it later, and he said, "Well, son, some people just feel that way, and you are not going to change their mind."

I: So, your father wasn't prejudiced at all.

JW: No. . . . In fact, one of the first people I can remember ever knowing in my life was Buddy Hayes, who was a black man, the shoeshine man, who had a band, played the trumpet. Where I had my haircut. . . .

I: Was that downtown?

JW: Yes, U of A Barber Shop downtown. . . . And I've known him my entire life. Probably the first human I ever knew, I don't know.

I: We have also asked people why they think that the integration worked so well here, as opposed to say, Little Rock?

JW: One of the incidents that I remember about the Little Rock thing, on the front page of *Look* magazine there was a picture of a boy running down the steps of Central High in Little Rock carrying an American flag and just raising all kinds of cane and that boy was Satid Spiro Brumus. He, Satid, worked for my dad as a delivery man, worked his way through college, and one of the reasons that he had to work his way through college, I was told, is because his father, who I understand was very wealthy, disinherited him over the whole incident. So, when he came to go to the University, he had to work his way through college. I will never forget that.

For one thing, I have been told, and I suppose it is true, they said, "Well, you all didn't have any problems because there were just a few blacks and you all knew them all and you [were] basically at ease with each other." So we just didn't have any problems, at least none that I ever knew of. But you know that I can understand that the heavier concentration of the population being, say in Little Rock, or Fort Smith even, that it might be, that might have generated in itself some friction. I suppose that is why we never had any problems. . . .

I think that Bull Hayes, after his career in school here, did a small college bit and then became a coach. . . . One of the things that I remember about him was his tremendous leg strength—oh my word—that was the strongest human being that I ever knew. And yet he was a very gentle person and someone that wouldn't hurt a fly.

STEVE CUMMINGS

Steve Cummings, a native of Fayetteville, was a student at Fayetteville High School in the initial years of desegregation and a star athlete who played football with William "Bull" Hayes, an outstanding black member of the Fayetteville High School team.

INTERVIEWER: Did you graduate in 1958?

STEVE CUMMINGS: No, I graduated in '59.

I: What position did you play on the football team?

SC: I played left halfback. Bull Hayes played fullback. Bobby Hudgins was the right halfback, and Jimmy Shreve was the quarterback, and Hoover Evans was the big end. And we had a coach that had put in a new formation. They use this a lot now. There was an overload. Here was Hoover, here was another, and then there was one, two, three, four. Bull played not more than three feet behind the quarterback. I stood behind here and Hudgins here. A lot of the plays were snapped between Peavine's [Jimmy Shreve's] legs.

I: There was the center, then behind him Jimmy Shreve, the quarterback, then behind him Bull Hayes.

SC: Yes, the center, Peavine, and then Bull. And some of these plays just went right directly to Bull and he would hit here and then here. . . .

I: Was this still Coach Vandergriff?

SC: No, this was Coach . . . [Clayton Spencer].

I: What we were trying to do is talk to people about the first year that the high school was integrated, but you were not there in that year?

SC: No, I was not.

I: But you were there when the athletes really started playing?

SC: I was there when the first black athlete really became famous.

I: Now, you call him Bull Hayes; what was his name?

sc: I think it was William Hayes.

i: And you said that he should have been all state and certainly all-district, but he was neither one. Everybody else on the team was all-district except him. Everybody.

sc: Except him. And then we had the two all-state players.

i: And that was the only year in the high school's history that the football team has gone undefeated?

sc: The only undefeated team, and if you go over to the gym, in the trophy case you will see a new picture that has been put up, and it says the only undefeated football team in Fayetteville High School history. And it has every player in this picture, all sitting together. Then it has a separate picture of Peavine and Hoover Evans, the two all-state players. You go over there and you can see the big picture, and Bull is in the picture, and maybe one or two other black players.

i: Tell me the story about the game.

sc: It was the seventh game of the season. Fayetteville High School was undefeated, and we realized that we had a chance to go undefeated if we could win the last three games—it had been an awful week prior to this game in terms of players having colds—several were in the hospital. Basically, when we arrived in Joplin, Missouri, on Friday night, most everybody was sick. Joplin was rated number three in the state of Missouri. We did not play well in the first half. On the last play of the first half I ran the ball forty yards and was tackled at the one-yard line, then the end of the half came . . . and the temperature was zero. So we go into the half and it is six to zero, Joplin. We come back out in the second half and we don't play well. And all of the sudden we find ourselves in a situation where there is only about four minutes to go in the fourth quarter, and it is still six to nothing and we are in terrible territory. And the boy, Pete Jenkins, is the punter. What actually happened was, we had the ball on about the twelve-yard line and Bull fumbles and they recover the ball. We hold them four plays; we get the ball, and then Jenkins goes back to punt, and the punt is blocked. That means that Joplin has the ball on our ten- or twelve-yard line, first down. Time is running out. Joplin ran four straight plays, and we held them and took over on about the five-yard line. We ran two plays and I fumbled. Joplin recovered the ball. They have first down on about the eight-yard line and four plays to go and time is running out. We held them that next four plays. So, we held them eight straight plays within the fifteen-yard line. We huddle and Bobby

Hudgins and I had on garden gloves that were cut at the fingers because of the cold. Peavine, the quarterback, in very clear language, calls a play and he looks at Bull's hands, and me and Bobby and Bull are standing like this [with hands on knees], and Peavine says to Bull, he knows that Bull has fumbled once, but he forgets that I fumbled the second time. He looks at Bull's black hands and says, "Bull, take your goddamned gloves off." And then Bull put out his hands in front of Peavine and says, "Peavine, I ain't got no gloves on." The next play, Peavine threw a seventy-eight-yard touchdown pass to Hoover Evans. We kicked the extra point with a minute to go in the ballgame. We beat them seven to six. We got on the bus and came home and finished our season undefeated.

I: That's great. Was that the hardest game that you played that year.

SC: Yes.

I: You said that Bull just played offense?

SC: Just played offense and it was his first year in football. He weighed 194 pounds and was 6 feet and ran the hundred in about 10.4. And his father was Buddy Hayes, who was a Negro who was known by everyone in town. He went on to the University of Nebraska, I think that he graduated . . . then he became involved in . . .

I: He was the athletic director at a youth club in a city.

SC: Then he died of sickle-cell anemia . . . then what you need to tie in there to is that that particular year, the season of 1957, there was also one other undefeated team in Arkansas and that was Little Rock Central. . . . They were undefeated. When it came down to the final vote as to who was number one in the state, Fayetteville was dismissed entirely because of Bull Hayes. And Bull was not elected all-state, nor was he elected all-district.

I: How did that make the team feel, when they found out that they were not voted number one? Were you angry at the system, or . . .

SC: Mad at the system, very mad at the system, but I was always against the system. We had great crowds. . . . Bull was the first of his kind. Remember that none of the other schools had integrated and the Little Rock crisis had not begun, it was the next year . . . it was not so much a big issue then because no one talked about blacks. Fayetteville was a different town. They used to transport the blacks to Fort Smith to go to school until '54. And there was never any problem between blacks and whites . . . it was the beginning of integration. . . . You talk about the one great touchdown, it was against Springfield Central, Bull ran it ninety yards for a touchdown, and we beat them twenty-one to nothing.

PART THREE

COMMUNITY

LEADERS

THELMA R. ENGLER

Thelma R. Engler, a native of Kansas and the wife of a University of Arkansas professor of agriculture, was active in the Presbyterian Church, state president of United Church Woman, and chairperson of the board of directors of the Arkansas Council on Human Relations.

INTERVIEWER: Start, Mrs. Engler, and talk about the organization you were associated with.

THELMA R. ENGLER: Arkansas Council on Human Relations. It was a statewide organization. I guess you know that.

I: I don't know much about it really.

TE: Well, this was related to the Southern Regional Council, and the Southern Regional Council was set up by, I've forgotten who it was. . . . Its purpose was to find out what the situation was [in race relations] and, if possible, to make some suggestions for remedies, and that was what was behind all this. We got reports from many towns . . . of what was being done in the matter of integration and, boy, it was precious little, practically nothing.

I: What year was the organization founded here in Fayetteville?

TE: I'm not sure. I'm not sure what year I became associated with it, but it was very early on.

I: It says '63 here.

TE: Yes.

I: Now, the school, the high school, I know was integrated—

TE: '57.

I: Fall of '54.

TE: And that's the Little Rock one?

I: Here in Fayetteville. Was there any preliminary work done by you or anyone that you became associated with in that school integration decision here?

TE: Back then, the only way to do it was so quietly that no one knew it was going on. No publicity of any kind, because publicity was deadly.

I: Now, was the organization in existence here in '54?

TE: We did not have a local council on human relations. The only vehicle we had was through the Arkansas Council on Human Relations, and they had a tremendous executive secretary who could come to communities and help them if they needed it.

I: Who was that?

TE: Oh, gosh, I can't even remember his name. He had been a Methodist preacher for a long time. I haven't seen or heard of him for years. I doubt if he's even living now.

I: He was executive secretary of this organization then. The *Brown* decision came down in May of '54, and then four days later the board here voted to integrate the high school. What memories do you have of that? First of all, are you originally from this area?

TE: No, but we've been here since '37.

I: What memories do you have of that particular period, that particular decision?

TE: My children were not old enough to be in high school then, so I knew very little about what was going on as far as the integration was concerned. I don't know how the kids were treated. I know a little about the University but not the high school. My husband was a university professor.

I: Do you have any recollections of how the community reacted to the decision? Was there any uproar about this?

TE: Well, it wasn't looked upon favorably, naturally. I can remember in the early days when I was connected with the Arkansas Council—some way or other my name became *persona non grata*. And I had people who would go across the street when they saw me coming rather than meet me and speak to me. So you see, people were pretty cool to anybody who was supporting integration. It was a no-no. But I think Fayetteville was far more liberal than most of the towns in Arkansas because of the University.

I: One thing that struck me was this was a rather matter-of-fact decision by the board. Just looking back through the documents and talking to some of the school board members, there doesn't seem to have been any great outcry or community pressure or demonstrations or anything of that sort.

TE: But I was president of the United Church Women of Arkansas about that time, and we had the convention here, and the meetings were held in the Episcopal Church. And we had a person that we

wanted to speak to us on this integration thing. It was the president
[of the University], John Caldwell. He wanted to know whether the
press was ever present.

I: I saw an article in a school—*Southern School News*—I believe
that was April of '55.

TE: That'd be about right.

I: There was a meeting at the Episcopal Church, and there was a
reporter from the *Northwest Arkansas Times*—

TE: Yes, Ted Wylie.

I: Right, right. I remember that name. And he wanted to cover
the meeting.

TE: When Caldwell, who was in a tenuous position at the University
—when I asked him to talk on the University and integration, he
said, "I just can't do that if the press is going to be there." And I said,
"Well, the press has never bothered to come near us, so I would
doubt very much if anybody would be there." And we did not
announce it. How Ted Wylie found out we were meeting, I don't
know, but anyway, he showed up after the meeting started, so there
was no chance to talk with him and tell him that we'd rather not
have it reported. And so, I—we stood our ground and said if this is
to be reported—Dr. Caldwell cannot freely say what he intended to
say. And so Ted got mad, and did he go out the door and bang it.

I: Did he mention it in the paper?

TE: He wrote a nasty article. . . . It said something about "supposed to be open to the press," but they didn't want them in there
because of the topic. We knew that he couldn't—we knew he
[Caldwell] wouldn't dare speak on that because the subject was just
too taboo in the state yet. Anybody that integrated was like the
young man in Little Rock who took such a strong stand that his
business was boycotted. And it would have been Caldwell's death
politically to give the speech that he gave about growing up in,
where was it, Georgia, somewhere down there, and how he felt constrained by the fact that he could play with his little boy friend, who
was black, but when they got up to junior high age, he had to discontinue his friendship.

I: He could play with them when he was young.

TE: Yeah, as a younger child, yes, it was perfectly all right.

I: But there was some mention—there was an article in the
paper. I was looking through the *Northwest Arkansas Times* on
microfilm the other day trying to find it. There was an article there
about this meeting.

TE: Yes, Ted wrote something about it, but I don't—it was the fact that we were limiting freedom of information; that was the essence of the thing.

I: What—did you say this was the church women's organization?

TE: United Church Women of Arkansas. It was a statewide organization.

I: Now, was it across denominations?

TE: Yes. It was a national organization, and the national organization had, in turn, set up state organizations, and then local towns had them. It was an attempt to get the churches to be less critical of each other and to work together for common projects.

I: What church did you belong to?

TE: I was Presbyterian. Some of the more—the older churches just couldn't see it. The Presbyterian and Christian churches and Episcopal churches were the most liberal when it came to accepting blacks in their congregations and in their schools and towns.

I: That's another thing I wanted to ask you. How influential were the churches in the community in smoothing the process of integration?

TE: Not as a church organization. Now, the ministerial association couldn't do anything like this because it included too many of the fundamentalist churches who wouldn't go along—but organizations like the United Church Women—but I don't think we carried any clout particularly, except that we kept the idea of accepting everybody as the ideal.

I: What factors, do you think from your experience, made this a more moderate process in Fayetteville than it was in many places across the South?

TE: Well, the University had to have a lot of influence because the faculty was from everywhere, and that made for a very liberal outlook. And, of course, the president at that time was—he had no prejudices at all that were visible.

I: He was a Southerner?

TE: Yes, he was, I think, from Georgia if I remember correctly.

I: You talked about the churches. How about the business community?

TE: Well, of course, you know at that time public opinion was such that business couldn't be too bold, because it was deadly. Now, when this dog-and-pet-food man in Little Rock took such a strong stand for integration, he was boycotted. And when he had an ad in the *Gazette*, the little pickup trucks in south Arkansas had a little sign in the back window saying, "*Gazette* ad, too bad." You've heard that one before.

I: No.

TE: Well, that's how constrained the business people were, because of public opinion. It was hard going. I had people—did I tell you this?—that would walk across the street rather than speak to me?

I: Yes.

TE: Because they thought that I was too radical.

I: This was as late as the sixties.

TE: Yes.

I: Another thing I wanted to ask you to comment on was the effect of numbers. How did the fact that there were only six students who were admitted that year, '54, how significant was that, you think?

TE: Well, I wonder how many of them wanted to come. Now, you see, they were going to Fort Smith—

I: Right. And Hot Springs.

TE: And Hot Springs and even some to Wichita, Kansas.

I: Oh, is that right?

TE: One family here had relatives in Wichita, and they sent their kids of high school age—they sent them to Wichita for school.

I: Did the small numbers have an effect on the lack of problems?

TE: The small numbers were hard on the kids, the black kids. They were pretty much shunned, I believe.

I: I guess what I wanted to know is, did the fact that there were very few of them—did that serve to mollify the white reaction, that there were only six students?

TE: I'm not at all sure that would be the case, because they've got a toe in the door, you know, and that's just what we didn't want. I'm not speaking personally.

I: Was your organization involved in the integration of the one-through-six grades later—Lincoln School integration?

TE: Not directly.

I: So this organization, the Arkansas Council on Human Relations, Fayetteville chapter, only came into being in the—

TE: It was never very active. Well, one time we had a Southern speaker come and talk to us, and we had an invitation-only banquet because you just didn't open things like that for the public because of the backlash you would get.

I: Southern, you mean a Southern black speaker?

TE: No, she was white. What was her name, Smith [Lillian Smith]? What was her first name? I can't remember, but her last name was Smith, and I think she was from either Alabama or Georgia.

I: She came to speak about integration?

TE: Well, she came to speak about her feelings as a child in knowing that segregation was wrong, that it wasn't intended that races would fight each other like that, and she just felt it was an evil thing and needed something to be done about it.

I: This is a council on human relations meeting she's speaking to?

TE: Yes.

I: So you didn't have to worry with the press on that one.

TE: No, it was closed. We didn't announce it. It was by invitation only. You had to do things like that back then because there were others—we had a guy here in town who was a radical against integration. Boy, he just raised [cane?] over any little favor that the blacks got. It was real bad. I got so that I walked across the street from him when I saw him, too, because I knew he was going to get me caged in. He'd talk forever, and he was so vicious. But now, where there's one like that, there's a lot of exactly the opposite.

I: Well, if you had to prioritize the reasons why desegregation went smoother here than it did so many other places, what would you cite as being the most important?

TE: One is the fact that this is a university community, which means it's more liberal in its stance. Two, there were so few blacks, far fewer than there are now, that the whites would not be overwhelmed by them. I think that was the two factors that were most important in getting them accepted.

I: What was the extent of your contact with the black community in that time? Did this church organization, United Church Women, include blacks?

TE: It did include them. Yes, and we had meetings down there at their churches and, you know, I think we set up a little kindergarten for the working women—nursery, maybe, is a better word—for the working women, and it was set up in the Methodist church, black [St. James] Methodist church, so the women could come and leave their children with some supervision. Now, that's—I'd forgotten all about that, but that comes to the surface now. I don't remember how we did it—whether it was somebody paid or whether it was volunteers or what.

I: If you had to pick outstanding personalities in the community who contributed to the smoothness of the transition, who comes to mind?

TE: Oh, I don't think of anybody that was way out front. The school board, I think, did a real good job, considering the feeling of the times.

I: In what way?

TE: They, their entering of these [black] kids into the school was just sort of a matter-of-fact thing. No big thing. There were not very many of them. If there had been a lot of them, it would have been different, but there were so few, I don't remember how many, but there were—

I: Six, I think, initially.

TE: Is that what it was? I knew it wasn't many. And I didn't know any of those kids, so I never got their viewpoint, how they were treated.

I: Any other recollections you have of that time or of this period that you could share with me?

TE: Well, I'll say that it was very exciting, and I sure would have hated to have missed it. And I feel like that a lot of the good people in this state really stuck their necks out to make it go smoothly. And some of them had an economic cost. . . . Has anyone mentioned to you that the leadership in the black community all came from the women?

I: No.

TE: There was not a single [African-American] man that was involved anywhere in trying to get blacks and whites together, but there were a number of wonderful women.

I: Why is that, you think?

TE: Well, I don't know. I think one reason is that women are natu-rally the nurturers of the family, I think. But I can't tell you a single Negro that took any active part.

I: So apparently by 1963, Lincoln was still operating as a segre-gated [black] school.

TE: I don't remember.

I: Did you ever have any contact with the school personnel, either Mr. Blossom or Mr. White?

TE: Not [Wayne] White, but [Virgil] Blossom. When the Little Rock schools were going to integrate, the Arkansas Council on Human Relations board had him come—this was a meeting in

Little Rock—had him come to speak to us about the integration in Little Rock and how they should go about it. He did not want one word of this broadcast. He wanted to have these kids show up without anybody knowing anything about it. Well, we warned him that that would be nothing but trouble and asked him to investigate Louisville's integration process, which went smooth as silk, because the Louisville school board held prior meetings with teachers, with the public, and what have you, and they all knew what was going on, and they did not feel threatened. But Blossom said, "No, we cannot do that." He said if we let it be known before the day that this happens, we'll have trouble. We told him he was doing it exactly backwards.

I: Are you talking about Fayetteville or Little Rock?

TE: In Little Rock, yes. The integration of the nine down there. See, that fell like a bolt of lightning on the city, and you know that was a terrible, terrible time. And Blossom was responsible for it, really, because if he had taken the advice of the council and contacted the Louisville people to know how well it went there, he could have avoided all that, I think. I think that we would have accepted integration in Arkansas as easily as Kentucky did.

I: He had been very successful here [Fayetteville] as I understand it. He laid the framework for integration here.

TE: Yeah, but you see this is different from Little Rock.

I: Different situation.

TE: I expect I'm the only person that knows about that meeting we had with him in Little Rock. There were just a very few of us there to try to give him advice. Members from various schools and so on. But he had made up his mind, and he was going to have no publicity about it at all. So it was dropped like a bolt of lightning.

I: Were you working? Were you employed at this time?

TE: No, I've never been employed after I was married. Wasn't I lucky?

I: I was wondering if you had run into any opposition at work.

TE: Well, my husband was on the faculty at the University. That made some difference. If he'd been a businessman, it might have been different. So I don't say that I was brave at all. I just had lucky circumstances.

ELAINE O. MCNEIL

Elaine O. McNeil, a native of Connecticut, is a retired professor of sociology who first became involved in the study of race relations in the 1930s. Moving to Fayetteville in 1953, she was active in improving race relations and in efforts to eliminate institutional segregation in the town.

ELAINE O. McNEIL: Well, under Jim Crow segregation, you had blacks, correct that, we called them Negroes—other people called them colored people or niggers, you know—but Negroes were what the common term was in those days. And I had gotten interested in race relations, first in the 1930s. I was one of the very rare whites who got interested, and it was just by coincidence. I had a WPA research job in Chicago, and the job was—I had my master's degree then, and my field was social stratification, basically, and I had written a thesis on the society girl, which attracted national publicity. But I was very interested in the effect of class on opinion and orientation and so on. That's what sociologists do, you know, with stratification.

So, I was very interested and applied for a civil-service–like job with the WPA. It was a white-collar research project. And I was a supervisor in Chicago, and my work contributed to a book called *Black Metropolis,* published in 1942. I had ended up running the whole project, actually, for a while, and I was a minority. . . . I'm trying to explain why I was so interested in blacks. I was a minority white in that group. It was 90 percent black, 10 percent white, so I got the feeling of being, first, in the minority. I also began to identify with blacks, so much so that I regarded them as my people. I never thought of myself as a white person. I always regretted I couldn't pass as black, you know, because we were that close. I associated with them every day, went to parties, and so on. And then I moved to Louisville and found the situation quite different.

INTERVIEWER: And your home was—where was your home?

EM: My home was in Connecticut.

I: Connecticut.

EM: Right, and we had very, very few blacks in Waterbury, Connecticut. I did know a few, but I had no feelings about race at all. I had taken a course or two about race relations in my work at the University of Chicago in the sociology department there, so I knew a little bit about it. But I didn't really begin to identify with black problems until this experience in Chicago. And I wrote some monographs and edited some other monographs and so on. And then, of course, the war came, and I taught a course—after the war—I taught a course on the Negro in America, one of the first courses by that title that wasn't being taught at a black school by a black.

I: This was at Chicago.

EM: No, this was at Coe College in Cedar Rapids, Iowa. The dean had asked me to teach a course, and I suggested this course, and he was very doubtful, but he said, "Let's try it." And it went over quite well. . . . I also had already written some articles about black-white relations. So anyway, I was ready when I came to Fayetteville to work, you know, I was already interested in this, very long before I ever came to Fayetteville.

I: You came to Fayetteville what year?

EM: 1953. And shortly after I got here, I met a number of other faculty wives, and I was thinking about this earlier—the significance of the fact that women didn't work in those [days]—married women, very few married women worked for pay. Back in those days, I had had a very good job, but when I got married, I quit working—did volunteer work from then on or joined organizations. So that various organizations, women's organizations, were very active in that period, much more than they are now. Because today, women are working, and they don't have time.

I joined this group, which was an informal group, and it was mostly faculty wives, and they were mostly interested in international affairs. We were very concerned about things like nuclear warfare. This was 1953, '54. Some of us got to talking about foreign students. Then we starting talking about black, Negro students, black students, because, as you know—I guess you know—the University of Arkansas was the first school—I think it was the very first Southern school—to desegregate its law school without a lawsuit. That was in 1948. So, there were a few black law students around. And then the University started admitting other black students but kept them segregated in segregated housing. And some of us, being interested in students, thought that was wrong. The University shouldn't be segregating these students that it had admitted. So we were already working in this area.

Of course, the public schools were segregated. . . . In the first place, we had less than 1 percent black population in those years. I guess we still do—a very small black population—a very small percentage. So, obviously, there weren't very many children involved. And they had a black school; when we came here in 1953, there was a black school, which had, I believe, nine grades.

I: That was Lincoln, correct?

EM: Lincoln School, yes, over in what we used to call "Tin Cup." . . . A lot of black kids probably dropped out after nine grades. But the ones whose parents wanted them to go on to high school were sent—and I don't know when it started—they were sent away. They were sent to Hot Springs or Fort Smith or someplace where there was a black school, and they were paid. . . . So that, of course, was an expense for the schools. And it was really kind of odd, but they actually had to go out of town simply because there were so few blacks in this area. And, but we got interested, this group, which called itself the World Affairs Group. . . . We met, I think, about twice a month. . . . And it was a rather small group, and it was almost all faculty wives in philosophy and art, and of course, I was a faculty wife then. I was not teaching. Oh, there were a couple of scientists' wives. . . . And we talked about world affairs. But then we got interested in foreign students. Then we got interested in the black, Negro students, and particularly we were instrumental in, I think—and again I don't have any record and I have no detail—we finally got the University to stop segregating the black students. . . . They were not living in the dorms. They were living in a little house all by themselves, what few we had. . . .

And that gave us the idea that there ought to be blacks—why should we send blacks [away] to high school, the very few that were here. There were three or four or five each year. Why was the school board spending money on them—spending taxpayers' money to send them off someplace? And so that gave us the idea of integrating the high school. So we discussed it. Now, I happened to know . . . the school superintendent [Wayne White]. . .

The first was the high school, which was kind of odd, but it was—well, they [the school board] gave the reason—to save money. This was the reason. I wish I had a clipping or could remember it, the exact quotation, because they made a little statement. They were desegregating the high school—I think it was something like to save money . . . and because it was right. Or because it was the law of the land, something like that. But the major reason was to save money. And there were only maybe six students involved. It was very, very quietly done. There were no demonstrations. Most people didn't even know it had happened, except the kids in the high school.

I: One of the things we're trying to determine is why it went so smoothly here as opposed to other places.

EM: Well, I don't know why. Of course, I got to know Wayne White, the superintendent, very well. We wrote him letters. We wrote letters—two or three of us in this World Affairs Group— wrote him letters just as private citizens and to all the school board members, urging them, I guess, to desegregate the high school. I don't know what the letters said. And they all answered and said, you know, thanks for your letter or whatever. And then I got a letter, which I don't have, of course, from Wayne White, because I apparently had written him also. And then later on, I went on a trip with Wayne White to some place—I don't know where it was, perhaps Oklahoma—it was probably some nearby place, because we went for the day and had a workshop, and Wayne bragged about the success of the desegregation process in Fayetteville, and I was there to back him up and add information because I knew quite a bit about it. I had written a book on desegregation, and I've had articles and papers published. . . .

So I knew quite a bit about tactics and how to go about things. So everything was very, very quiet. Wayne White never knew who we were. When I was talking to him, at one point, well, he knew there was a group of women in town—I think someone had written a letter saying there could be a lawsuit if we didn't desegregate, but I can't remember exactly what the letter said even. But there was a hint of a threat there.

I: There are some records of this human relations—what's the, I don't know the exact . . .

EM: Oh, Arkansas Council on Human Relations.

I: Right, there are some records of that in Special Collections [of Mullins Library, University of Arkansas]. Are you saying the letter emanated from that group?

EM: No, no. It emanated from the World Affairs Group, which nobody knew about, which was this very private group.

I: So the letters were anonymous?

EM: No, the letters were always signed that we sent.

I: You said he didn't know who you were.

EM: No, he just assumed that we were a large, powerful group, not realizing that we were a tiny, little group. And what amused me as a sociologist—I know that when you have a social movement, it's very important to get people of prestige to be spokespeople, to present the public front for the group while the real workers can be anybody. And I was very amused by Wayne White because he just assumed that Mrs. So-and-so was active in that group. This was a very prominent woman, a friend of mine—she never had anything to do with the group, but I never told him, because I thought, well, if he thinks she's involved in it, I'm not going to tell him she isn't, you know—why should I? We were just a bunch of liberals who were interested in world affairs. We were interested in peace, nuclear warfare, and all kinds of issues besides desegregation. Desegregation was just one of them. The Fayetteville Council on Human Relations was formed later on, but by that time the schools were desegregated. But then we worked on—they worked on things like desegregating the swimming pool, desegregating the theaters, and so on . . .

We knew—this little World Affairs Group, I met through a couple of members—we had a social affair one night, and I met the two black school teachers. And so then I invited them—we all invited them—to come to the World Affairs Group. So they came—one of them I've lost track of completely. The other one's name was Minnie Dawkins.

I: Yes, I was going to mention her. Was she the principal at Lincoln School?

EM: Yes, yes, and she taught—well, she was principal and taught two or three grades also. . . . Fayetteville was very, you know, very quiet . . . I think having had the very quiet law school desegregation probably set the pattern. Nothing happened.

I: What other factors do you think had an influence on the smooth transition? Do you think it was the cost factor, was it the fact that there were very few numbers of blacks, was it influence of the University, was it the impact of churches or civic leaders, or was it just civic-minded school officials?

EM: I don't think the civic leaders were particularly involved. I

think we had an active—you know, we still do have a very active
civic life in Fayetteville. It's small enough—well, it's a large university in a small town. I had come from a large town with a small college, and the small college did not affect the community. I came
directly from Cedar Rapids—oh, I had been one year in Evanston
also, at Northwestern, but at Coe College, that's a small school, you
know, under a thousand students in a large town, Cedar Rapids.
The college had very little effect on that town. Came here, to a town
which was then, I think, around twenty thousand or so. And it [the
University] was five thousand or six thousand. Of course, the numbers have gone way up since, but we are still a relatively very large
college for the size of the town. And I think that has an impact on
the town. In the first place, you get a very cosmopolitan group of
people. You have scholars coming from all over the world, so people
are exposed to a lot of [different peoples and ideas]. The town is not
provincial the way many towns in Arkansas would be. So, I think
that's part of it, the impact, which may be kind of indirect even, but
then you have—I say at that particular time you did have these well-
educated women who had time on their hands. So they were frequently behind [civic reforms and improvements]—well, this is
true in all kinds of civic things. The women founded the library in
this town. Well, it's not just in this town—all over the country in
that period. Educated women who didn't have anything to do
because they weren't allowed to work. That would disgrace their
husband or something back in those days. So they had a lot of
energy, a lot of ideas, and a lot of influence. . . .

    I: If you were going to prioritize the factors that made the inte-
gration of the school in Fayetteville go more smoothly than other
places, what order of preference would you assign?

    EM: Well, I imagine, probably, the very small number of blacks.
So whites never felt threatened. You know, if you had a Ku Klux
Klan rally or something—but that's silly. We knew these people, and
they were less than about 1 percent of our population. And they had
been here for a long, long time. So I imagine, from a large viewpoint, it's probably that. And then, from a more micro aspect, I
imagine it's the personnel involved. Some of the people. And you
may be right, you know, [Virgil] Blossom—see, I wasn't here when
Blossom was here, and I later got very prejudiced against Blossom
because of the trouble we had in Little Rock with him in that [1957]
mess, and he was not very cooperative at all in many ways. He was

doing things that we thought he shouldn't be doing, and we wondered what had happened. In fact, I think I heard people who knew him here saying, "What happened to Virgil [in Little Rock]?" Of course, he was in a very different situation down there with 22 percent or so black students, maybe higher than that, I don't know. Twenty-two percent and that's statewide for black population, and a rather high percentage in Little Rock. So it was a different situation and more volatile.

I: The impression I got from talking to these people was that he got the job in Little Rock partly as a result of the work he had done here.

EM: Well, that's possible. But I wasn't aware of any preparatory work particularly, but, now, maybe they're talking about this cooperation on the part of Lincoln School with the other schools.

I: I think that's what they are talking about.

EM: Yes, that would be something he would have done. He would have had to be involved in that. But I wasn't here then, so I don't know. I don't think I ever even met the man.

I: But you think numbers are important and cost was important. The University influence was important, you think. And the—

EM: I think the fact that everything had gone smoothly. All the desegregation efforts in the University had worked out, and there wasn't any—I can't think of any really important opposition. We never had a [white] citizens' council. Of course, that formed in '55, '56. We never had one here that I'm aware of. I think I would have known it if there had been. There were a few malcontents who wrote to the newspapers; they might have objected, but . . . there were not [large] numbers involved and nobody of any great prestige.

I: That's the impression I got. I talked to a former school board member who said that he never felt any kind of threat to his business or loss of any personal friendship, no kind of pressure exerted. I saw the minutes of the board meeting. It was very matter-of-fact.

EM: When they decided to do it? Was that five days after the [1954 Supreme Court] decision? I knew it was almost immediately. And, I think, maybe I even talked to Wayne White about it, because I would see him every now and then and discuss things with him.

I: Coming from New England and then from the Midwest, were you surprised at the ease with which these events took place in Fayetteville?

EM: You mean as far as blacks were concerned?

I: Right.

EM: I wasn't. I just thought there was such a small population, but I was very gratified that they were doing what they were doing in the University and then in the schools. But I think the tiny population makes a difference—and the fact that it's a large university in a small town. And there weren't any really prejudiced people in the power structure as far as I know. You know, they were willing to go along. . . .

I: You made mention a while ago. Something that people wouldn't want known—people wouldn't want their affiliation with this organization known, this World Affairs Group?

EM: Oh, well, probably not at the time, but as I say, most of them are gone now. It was kind of an undercover organization, and I think that that's why we were effective. We did a lot of different things, and nobody ever knew who was doing it. And we didn't make a big deal out of it either. I'll have to tell you one thing. I've already mentioned this in a speech that I did at the women's festival, so I guess it's safe to mention it again. We decided shortly after the sit-ins in Greensboro to try to desegregate Woolworth's here too. Because that [Greensboro] was a Woolworth's sit-in, as you may remember. We had a Woolworth's downtown that had a lunch counter, and as far as we knew never had served blacks. Blacks never tried to go in there, I guess. We made these elaborate arrangements . . . we rehearsed, you know, to not lose our cool, to be nonviolent, and so on, and we would do it very quietly. We had two of our white members and, I guess, maybe the black schoolteachers—I don't know who the blacks were—but we had a couple of blacks and a couple of whites just meet down there in front of Woolworth's and just go in and sit down at the counter and order some ice cream or something. And they were served. You know, nothing happened. And it was the kind of thing that we were delighted by, that nobody cared. So that, kind of, is the way Fayetteville is, I think. And I don't know, there may be other incidents like that, but I don't know about them.

I: Is part of it geography, you think?

EM: Northwest Arkansas, right.

I: This was sort of a Unionist area going back to the Civil War.

EM: I think the town was divided, actually, during the Civil War. Was it more pro-Union?

I: Well, I think it was just a Unionist part of the state, because there wasn't that much obviously large-scale agriculture around here.

EM: Yes. It's partly that, I'm sure. Yes, we're so close to Missouri.

I: It's very atypical. It's not really a "Southern town" in many respects.

EM: No, no, I don't think so. In fact, when I came here, being as liberal on race as I am, I told everybody this is the only place in Arkansas I would be willing to live—when I saw—or heard—what the rest of the state was like, that it was very open, and I felt—I didn't feel uncomfortable here, as I did in Louisville. We lived in Louisville very briefly in 1940. It's a large town with a large Negro population, and I wasn't comfortable there. If I'd stayed there, I probably would have wanted to do something about all this because there was big segregation back in the 1940s.

I: Do you think if there had been sixty black students instead of six, the situation might have been considerably different?

EM: Oh, yes, I think so. But that's just common sense. But again, it might depend on how they did it and the timing and the presentation. The idea of saving money, taxpayers really like that. So, I thought that was very clever of them, but I think it was also one of the reasons they did it. They realized they could cut here.

LORRAINE B. BASHOR,
PHILIP S. BASHOR,
AND LODENE DEFFEBAUGH

Philip S. Bashor, born in Los Angeles and educated at Yale, joined the philosophy faculty of the University of Arkansas in 1960. His wife, Lorraine B. ("Lorrie") Bashor, was a native of Connecticut and a housewife. Both were active in various organizations, including the Fayetteville Community Relations Association, which pressed for the integration of the town's elementary schools. Lodene Deffebaugh, a native of Fayetteville and prominent in the town's African-American community, was a civil rights activist and key figure in the Fayetteville Community Relations Association.

INTERVIEWER: Let's start with what your role was and what you were doing in the period around 1954 when the high school was integrated, and then later I'd like to know about the Lincoln School [for black students]. *Brown* [decision] was in '54, and the high school integrated that fall, I believe. Is that right?

LODENE DEFFEBAUGH: Yes, because we had kids going to Fort Smith to school, and it was about nine of them. Of course, the school board paid for their expenses. OK, from '57 to '65, they integrated high school and junior high. Our kids—we [blacks] were still going to [a segregated] elementary school. We had a two-story building where the housing project now stands. That was the elementary school, which was from one through the sixth grade. And we were getting inferior teachers to come in and teach our kids. Our kids were integrated in high school and junior high during that time. I was president of the Lincoln School PTA, and we were getting inferior teachers to come in and teach our elementary kids. They would go—when they finished sixth grade, they would go to seventh grade. In elementary school they were four years behind the regular kids. And we became, you know, dissatisfied with the whole situation and started trying to get rid of the principal [Pearlie

Williams] we had there. She was in cahoots with the school super-intendent, who was Wayne White. He did not want integration any-way, but the junior high school and the high school were already integrated. He didn't want to start [integration] on the elementary level, so he had Pearlie, Pearlie Williams was her name. She fought us tooth and nail trying to keep the elementary school from being integrated.

I: She was the principal at the Lincoln School?

LD: She was the principal at Lincoln School. And I was the president of the PTA. This is when the human relations council [Fayetteville Community Relations Council] became effective for us. Now, we were already established on campus. This was a group of professors, lawyers, teachers, concerned citizens—white—that was working with the black community. So they became our allies, and I was trying to integrate Lincoln School. So we worked on that, I guess, about maybe two or three years. We got names, we had peti-tions, and got people that really wanted it so our kids would at least get a decent start, you know, before they started junior high. And we had formed committees in the human relations council. We were on the school committee. In the human relations council, we were trying to integrate the whole city of Fayetteville, so we had dif-ferent committees working. I was on the school committee. Then we had a committee for the swimming pool, a committee for the eating establishments, you know, everything, because we had to go at this thing in steps. It was bad back in those days, you know. So Phil [Bashor] and I were the main people with the school commit-tee, and we got the backup from the people in the community, organizations such as the League of Women Voters and Jaycees. We got all the churches—all the churches in Fayetteville. St. James Methodist, Central Methodist Church, University Baptist—trying to think of another church that was really supportive of us. Then we worked around, we had several meetings with the school board. The school board was—do you want names of people that were on the school board?

I: Sure, any names you give me.

LD: Henry Shreve, I think, was president of the school board.

I: I talked to William Morton. Was he on the school board too?

PHILIP S. BASHOR: Yes, Bill Morton.

LD: No, no, I don't remember William Morton, not when we were ... Hal Douglas, Hal Douglas. Hal is dead now. Henry Lee,

Hal Douglas, Tharel, George Tharel. Now, they were on the school board, and I think Henry Shreve was kind of wavery about it [integration]. He really didn't want it. But he would not block it, you know, if the school board really went for it. Wayne White was the superintendent of schools. He didn't want it. He did not want it at all. And Phil [Bashor] and I worked and worked and worked, and we finally had several meetings—I guess we just bothered and worried them to death, you know. And they finally decided we could start. They would integrate the elementary school, '65. Was it '65. . . . Must have been about '65. Anyway, the Washington School—all the elementary schools were opened to our kids. That's when we integrated. And, let's see, what else did we do?

PB: Well, basically, half of them went to Washington School and half of them went to Jefferson School, the black kids. A few went to Bates School.

LD: Bates. See, we were concentrated there in the community. That's the reason we didn't spread out and go, you know, go to all the schools because there wasn't any black people living in the neighborhood.

I: So the blacks were going to Lincoln. The whites were going to Washington and Jefferson.

LD: Right.

I: And then after integration, black students that had been going to Lincoln went . . .

LD: They went to Jefferson and Washington. Our kids were absorbed in the elementary schools. And our kids were already integrated in Woodland Junior High and the high school. We used to have two junior highs.

LORRAINE B. BASHOR: Hillcrest.

LD: Where the housing project there is now for the elderly. There used to be a high school—junior high. My kids went there. My kids went to Hillcrest and Woodland. OK. And, let's see, what else. Are you wanting to know some of the problems we had or just some of the—

I: I'll tell you one thing I'm interested in is that—the reason why the integration of the high school seemed to go so smoothly.

PB: The reason for the high school [integration] was financial.

LD: Financial reasons, as I was saying, you know, the kids that were coming out of Lincoln . . . they sent them to Fort Smith. And they paid their tuition and their vacation time home and this kind of thing. The class had got so big. The last class they had was nine, and paying tuition and room of board out of town didn't make sense. So they decided they'd just let them go to school here.

I: So you think that the motivation behind the high school integration then was financial more than anything else.

LD: Right, right.

LB: Because when she [Lodene Deffebaugh] went to school, they didn't even do that. She was just telling us she went to Atlanta, Texas, and the families paid their own way if they wanted to go to junior high school or on up. And she named a whole bunch of people who did that. And then, do you know the year that the school took on the responsibility, the financial responsibility of getting blacks into high school?

LD: I don't know. I don't remember. When I went to Atlanta, Texas, there wasn't any help, no support. I left home in 1939, I graduated and went to school in Texas the following fall.

LB: And they were completely on their own. Their families sent five dollars every three months. And that's how the kids did if they wanted further education, and a lot of wonderful people came out of that effort. But I don't know when they started paying for Fort Smith.

I: So some of the same people who were involved in the integration of the high school were not enthusiastic about the integration of the other schools.

LD: No, no, that's the reason it took so long to integrate the elementary school, '54 to '65.

I: So, Dr. Bashor, what was your involvement? How did you get involved in this?

PB: I came to the University, and shortly thereafter became connected with the Fayetteville Community Relations Association. That was the name, official name, "Fayetteville Community Relations Association," and worked with that group, a good bunch of people. Oh, we were integrating facilities, first of all, when I was there. Movie facilities, swimming pool, and others. Trying to bring these things about in a relatively peaceful, nonconfrontational way. Tried to avoid the violence which was occurring throughout the South, and particularly in Arkansas; of course, there is the aftermath of the Little Rock crisis and the governor's attitudes. He was trying to get elected. So there was deliberate use of racism going on in the state. And we were trying to counter that—a lot of people of good will. The picture I got of Fayetteville was that people were generally not against desegregation, but they weren't going to stick their necks out. So the Community Relations Association was the means by which some people would stick their necks out, break things of the past. It was after a couple of years that, as Lodene said, we really seriously started tackling the—finishing school integration. Technically, minimally, the University had been integrated, . . . but just minimally; the high school and junior high [had been integrated]. My understanding was that it was strictly a pragmatic issue, strictly financial.

LD: What had happened was that he [Reverend Jim Loudermilk of the Methodist Student Center] got to working with the community relations council. A lot of those professors' jobs were on the line, with them working with us. But who did they fire but Loudermilk. Loudermilk was gone. I mean they made it so.

PB: Yes, I think the University centers provided facilities for our meetings and moral support.

LB: The Presbyterian Center and the Methodist.

PB: Yes, the Presbyterian and Methodist, those were the only two centers.

LB: Dr. Loudermilk's Wesley Foundation and the Christian-Presbyterian Center on the corner of Storer and Maple [Streets]. They were all very central where we could meet.

PB: I don't recall any legal action. I think there was maybe the threat, the possibility, of legal action, but I don't recall any suit was prepared. Do you?

I: With everything going so smoothly with the high school, why was there such a big to-do about the elementary schools?

LD: I don't know. We never could figure that out.

LB: Well, I think that there were reasons. One of the reasons was that they knew the children were just that much younger as far as personal family reasons went for not having integration and for the same reasons that you can read about anywhere in the nation. What do you do when little tiny kids get together and start playing? And it's a much more personal day that they live, the little children. They thought that there were a lot of people who wouldn't want that. What they found out was that there wasn't much feeling at all. But that was what they were probably expecting. And they didn't want the little children to get together, and so it was better to wait until they got to junior high school. But in grammar school, they'd learn to like each other, and that was their worry about it. At least that's what I got. I mean, for instance, . . . the director of the training school at the University asked me to go find three families for three classrooms with a boy and a girl from each family for each classroom. And then she said, "Now, be sure that they're the nice families. If you go and get black families, I want the ones who won't cause any trouble and whose parents we can work with, who are upright and straight, you know, Girl Scouts and Boy Scouts." You know, I had to laugh when I came home and told Phil what the order was. Go find three families to bring in to the University training school. Our kids went to the University training school. Kindergarten, first, second, and third grade. Then they went on to the public school. But, you know, they wanted to pick and choose what kind of people, because they were afraid of trouble, basically.

I: It seems to me there had been so little trouble. In fact, in '54, everyone I talked to said there was just very little that went on in terms of protest or disorders of any kind that it's strange to me why, when you've already integrated one school and it went so smooth, why there's so much reluctance and so much of a gap there before you integrate the other one.

PB: The whole climate of the nation was different at the later point. Violence had erupted. Well, a major factor, though, I think, is that more people, a lot more pupils, were involved on the elementary level than in the senior high school.

LB: Well, Phil, when you and Lodene went to school board meetings and spoke, what happened? What resistance did you get from the school board? What talk was there? Can you remember?

PB: Well, I don't know, Lodene can speak about that. I remember she sort of blew her top at one meeting, I think. She's a real warrior type.

LD: Well, I wanted some answers. I knew they were dragging their feet. You know, it had been nearly five years. They were going to do it in six years. OK, five years passed and nobody doing anything. So this particular time when we went up, they thought I was sent in from the NAACP.

LB: They were always talking about . . . who was coming down from the North, who had to tell us what to do. They wanted to know who these people—wasn't it outside people? You know, the old story. If you're not a native, how could you possibly think that we were going to accept you to be part of integration [process].

LD: That's the time I threatened to call Bobby Kennedy. Hey, if you're not going to do it, you know. I did not have a number, ... but I told him this is what the committee decided, if you don't make a statement today, what we gonna do. I'm calling Bobby Kennedy. So the next day—I didn't have anything—but the next day, Wayne White called me at my job. I was doing domestic work then. He called me and told me they were going to integrate that fall.

I: This is fall of '64 or early 1965.

PB: That sounds right.

LD: See, what I'm trying to tell him—that the junior high and senior high were already integrated, so this lull in between here was when we were getting those bad teachers. And, OK, this is what bothered me, because the children, some of them never caught up. They just dropped out of school. So many of them just dropped out. It was hard on them when they went to the high school. Everybody had to readjust. The white kids had to adjust, and so did our kids. Some of them made it, and some of them didn't. They just dropped out.

LB: Do you think that Superintendent Wayne White was against integration of elementary schools?

LD: Sure he was.

LB: As a leader, he could always put his thumb on any action. You know, "I can work it so we don't have to do this. I can stall it for another year."

LD: He didn't want it anyway. The high school was going to be integrated. That's when Superintendent Virgil Blossom left, because he did not want black people over there at that school. And then Wayne White took over after Virgil left, and he put the clamps on—

LB: But he did allow the high school and the junior high school to integrate when he came.

LD: Well, it was already set up then.

I: OK, but now in '54 was when [grades] ten, eleven, and twelve were integrated. Junior high came in between elementary and the time that happened.

LD: Junior high. OK, high school was integrated in '54. It was right after the *Brown*—Then the next year after the high school was integrated, that next year they integrated, so that must have been '55, they integrated the junior high. We started integrating each year till we got it all, everybody was absorbed in the school system. You know, we had two different worlds going.

LB: Was there anyone for it [integration] on the school board?

LD: Henry Shreve was against it, I know. Hal Douglas was for it. And Tharel, guy that owned J. C. Penney, he was for it. 'Cause our kids played little league baseball together. They played together all the time anyway.

I: Why was Mr. White so opposed to it?

LD: Southerner. And why Wayne White anyway? You know, why these kind of people that you cannot fool.

LB: Well, they were brought here to do the job, and they did it. Hal Douglas, Henry Shreve, and who?

LD: I'm trying to think of somebody else . . .

LB: Now, you know Hal Douglas.

I: No, I don't.

LB: Hal Douglas was powerful. Hal Douglas was [U.S. Senator J.] William Fulbright's brother-in-law. And he had money and power here. So we had a little bit of an ally there. Did you ever go and talk to Hal Douglas about it?

PB: Seems to me like there was some communication, but I don't know.

LB: There were a lot of meetings as to how we could break the logjam. You know, put the coffee on when Lodene drives in, and then start trying to think of some new way.

LD: I'm trying to think—we were trying to keep trouble down, you know. We didn't want, and I really don't—basically, I don't think the school board wanted, they didn't want that publicity. You know, with the University being here.

LB: But the minute you threatened Bobby Kennedy, the next day—

LD: Yes, the only thing. I don't know what I was doing. I was just threatening people. I knew I was poor, but I had kids that I wanted to have a decent education. That's what my thing was. And they were trying to block me, and I didn't want to let them do it.

LB: And you were just the cleaning lady.

LD: Yeah, just the cleaning lady.

PB: Well, there was another element in the political climate at the time. It was the Act 10 crisis that affected the University. This was a legislative act, called Act 10. I don't know exactly what year, but it'd probably be '58 or '59, and—Maybe '57, it was an aftermath of the racial crisis generally, and it required that all employees of the state sign an affidavit, that they sign what memberships they belonged to. And they were trying to identify NAACP- and communist-affiliated organizations.

LB: They said they wanted to find the communists in the system and rout them out.

PB: It affected the faculty because all the faculty were employees of the state, and this created a crisis in academic freedom at the University. And there were some resignations over that. And the faculty fought Act 10 through the courts, raised money, and finally the Supreme Court declared this legislative act unconstitutional. That would be about 1960 or 1961.

LB: Was it still constitutional when we arrived in 1960?

PB: Yes, so in 1961, the Supreme Court banned it. That was an example of a very political thing that affected the Fayetteville community very directly.

I: You came in '60 from where?

PB: I was teaching at Lewis and Clark College in Portland, Oregon.

I: Are you from that area originally?

PB: Not really.

I: You said something a while ago about the fact that you were outsiders.

PB: Well, yes, we—Lorrie's from Connecticut; I was from California and educated in Yale University and teaching in Portland, Oregon, so we were not Southerners. And, of course, there were many faculty folks who were non-Southerners, non-natives.

LB: It did—it threatened higher education and anyone in it supporting Martin Luther King, integration, so part of the result of that was that one professor working in this organization was still being threatened in the sixties. His salary was on the line every year.

PB: Now, when was the Civil Rights Act passed?

I: There was one in 1964.

PB: 1964, well, I think that, locally, broke the back of the citizens here. So really, I think, that helped in integrating Lincoln School in 1965.

I: Yes, '65.

PB: So, the Civil Rights Act passed, the general facilities were either integrated or about to be integrated—about through the middle of the sixties. School integration was complete, and, in effect, community-relations work wound up at that point.

LB: Well, no, well, when did you integrate the theaters and restaurants?

LD: We integrated before the school.

LB: Because, you know, they would get a call, and it'd be from a restaurant. Phil and a friend would go out and would talk to the owners and try to appeal to them and to their better judgment that this was not going to cause trouble. But I thought the rest of the integration of the theaters was the most complicated and took the most restraint on your part, but you're not into that.

I: Ms. Deffebaugh, you had been involved in this process since when? You were here when the high school was integrated? You'd lived here all your life?

LD: Yes.

I: How long after the high school was integrated was it before you got involved in the process to integrate the elementary school?

LD: I started when my kids were in high school. My kids were in junior high—I don't know what year that was.

LB: How old is Jimmy now?

LD: How old is Jimmy? She's forty-nine.

LB: She's forty-nine. So when she went, she went to junior high school—

LD: She went to junior high and senior high.

LB: When she was fourteen.

LD: Yeah, fourteen, I guess.

LB: She was your oldest child.

I: You said also you got some support from the local congregations, some of the local organizations.

LD: Yes. The Jaycees, League of Women Voters. We met, that's all I did for about three years. I drove to a meeting almost every day and every night trying to get this elementary school dissolved.

I: So there was some support in the community for what you were trying to do? In the Fayetteville community.

LD: Yes, yes, I've got a clipping where the Jaycees were supporting us.

I: OK.

LB: The summer before the integration of the elementary schools, who was the group that established summer school at Lincoln in which Mrs. Thomason was the principal?

LD: It must have been my PTA. I was president of the PTA.

LB: Thelma Thomason became principal of Lincoln. The League of Women Voters and some churches thought that it would be a good idea to have some training that summer, so they did it at Lincoln. And then I had always worked with the nursery and the kindergarten that were in the Methodist church near the school. What's the name of the church—St. James—in the church basement. Her [Ms. Deffebaugh's] sister had started a nursery and kindergarten school there in the basement and was the first teacher. In the sixties, Christine Childress was the director, and I started working with her. And from 1960 to 1965, I had been taking the kindergarten-age children to our home and working with them on reading, writing, and arithmetic, and getting used to white teachers. They saw white people who came down to the kindergarten, but they hadn't gone away with them anywhere, and I started teaching them. So it was nothing new that summer when a lot of people started working in Lincoln School with them that summer. And I just went ahead and worked a little harder down there in the basement of the church. Our boys [the Bashors'] were just about that age, four and six. So they came to integrate the class. And I continued my work with them, and . . . from then on, I just went on working with every kindergarten age child who was going to go to an integrated school after 1965 to give them some readiness.

I: So, in general, you don't see that Fayetteville was that much different from any other of these towns in the South where a lot of this trouble was going on . . . in terms of racial understanding, racial harmony, things like that.

LB: It *was* different. There was *no* violence. But there was a considered attempt, I think by some people who didn't want violence, to keep it from happening, to keep pushing, never give up.

LD: Well, you know, I think the reason Fayetteville was sort of different was the black population here is so small. You didn't have—like in Fort Smith or Little Rock—the population was big and black folks would turn out. But we couldn't get our people to do this. It was only—just about ten or twelve of us that stood up.

I: Well, let me ask you this. It's something I've broached with some other people. The fact that there were only, I think, seven or nine students who integrated the high school that first year. Was the fact that the numbers were so small the contributing factor in why whites didn't really feel threatened by this small number of blacks, whereas they did feel threatened by the larger number in the elementary school. Is that a valid explanation or not?

PB: Yes, I think that's a valid explanation. I don't know about threatened, but, yes, threatened by change. In other words, the small number on high school level did not represent change, whereas a larger number, I think, did represent change. Now, there was a very difficult thing. You've already touched upon this with regard to elementary integration; mainly, what to do with the staff at Lincoln School. Well, they were under contract. I don't know if they had any tenure; I don't know if there was any tenure, but implicit within the Civil Rights Act or whatever these things were was that the staff should be integrated as well as the students. And once you bring in the elementary students, you're going to morally or perhaps legally have to hire some black teachers. These are going to be black teachers over white students in "white schools," so-called. So the people might be as much concerned about that as anything else. It's a violation that would not come out with just a small number of high school students, but that issue . . . was raised in connection with the integration of the elementary school. Now, it was solved as was mentioned by hiring the Thomasons.

LB: Thelma [Thomason] went to Butterfield [School], and Romey [Thomason] went to Woodland [School]. Romey has a degree from the University of Wisconsin.

LD: She's a classroom teacher. I believe she teaches fourth grade.

PB: Well, I don't know what the circumstances were when they were hired at Lincoln School, and they were—what shall we say— more highly capable or certified, I believe, than the usual Lincoln school teachers.

LB: And the others were let go.

LD: Right.

LB: What about the principal before Thelma? Who was that lady?

LD: Pearlie Williams.

LB: Pearlie Williams.

LD: We got her fired—this was Wayne White's administration. Because he and Pearlie were the ones keeping Lincoln from being integrated. . . .

LB: And you pushed to get her fired and brought in Thelma. And Thelma was for integration.

LD: Thelma and Romey were teachers with Pearlie Williams.

LB: And then they were for integration.

LD: Yes, well, they were there—they just didn't—

LB: They were never active. They were trying to hold onto their jobs.

LD: The black people did not want Pearlie Williams over their kids. We were for Pearlie in a lot of things, but nobody liked her in the community.

I: Why was that?

LD: Well, her attitude. She wasn't black.

I: So Pearlie Williams was a white person?

LD: What?

I: She was white?

LD: No, no.

I: Oh, you said she wasn't black. She wasn't black attitude-wise.

LD: Right.

I: OK.

LB: She was white-black. They brought in school principals who were not for integration.

LD: Well, OK, now, you know—do you remember Minnie Dawkins?

LB: Yes.

LD: Minnie Dawkins was the principal at Lincoln School. She was getting our kids ready to go to high school. She felt that they were going to be integrated. When our kids were integrated into the high school, Ms. Dawkins went to Philander Smith College in Little Rock. She was dean of Women at Philander for years. . . . Ms. Dawkins had been so good with our kids. That's another reason why it took so long for us to integrate. Ms. Dawkins was still there, and she was preparing the community. Everybody respected her. She was the principal at Lincoln there for about ten or twelve years or more. Very respectable in the community. She was helping us get ready for integration at the high school. She helped kids get ready for high school. She told the PTA that within five or six years, the elementary school's going to be integrated.

LB: You think if she had stayed, it would have happened.

LD: I think it would have. I think it would have happened way before then because she was for it anyway. Wayne White worked with Ms. Dawkins, can you believe that? The man had four or five sides of his mouth he talked out of. He'd tell us one thing, and he'd go do something else.

LB: Yes, that was right.

LD: But the ball really started rolling after the Thomasons went to [Lincoln School] and after we got rid of Pearlie Mae.

PB: At what point did Harry Vandergriff take over as superintendent? [By that time], the big work seemed to have been over, but I now think that we continued actively for several years.

LD: Oh, yes, oh, my goodness yes.

PB: After black kids were going to the elementary schools, there was always a question, a repeated question, about their treatment. And I remember there were some problems. The problems were particularly in high school, but we met—I met anyway—with Harry Vandergriff once or twice on handling incidents.

LD: Incidents.

PB: So I think incidents connected with integration continued for a couple of years, and the Community Relations Association had a role to play to investigate those to see that they were being treated fairly. I think to describe Vandergriff as being "fair minded" is very apt. . . . He wasn't any pushover. As I remember, he raised the question of how we were doing on the university level. "You're pushing the public schools," he said, "but I could push you on the University." And he was right.

LODENE DEFFEBAUGH

INTERVIEWER: Do you know how long Fayetteville had been paying black students to attend high school elsewhere?

LODENE DEFFEBAUGH: Let's see now, '39 is when they started sending them out of town.

I: How did the payment system work? Did the money go to the students or just directly to the school district from this school district?

LD: Now that I don't know. I couldn't tell you. I know the kids that went away, went to Fort Smith and Hot Springs. But I know when I left, when I went to Atlanta [Texas] to go to school, nobody paid. The school board didn't pay that.

I: And that was when?

LD: So that was in '39, and these kids, these kids that went to Fort Smith and Hot Springs—now this was years later.

I: The Fayetteville Community Relations Council—can you tell me something about that and its relation to the integration of the schools, what its role was?

LD: OK, the Fayetteville Community Relations Council was an organization that was founded through professors and their wives and the leaders in the black community. This organization was geared to help ease the integration of the public accommodations and school integration, swimming pools and this type of thing. And this was organized in sixty- . . . let me get this right now . . . because we were working along there with Martin Luther King. In fact, we had started possibly a year before Martin Luther King was really doing his thing. I'd say we started in sixty-, maybe about 1960, 'cause the schools were integrated.

I: The high school?

LD: High school was integrated.

I: That's when the order came down before the Supreme Court, and the high school integrated that year[1954].

LD: Well, now that order did not affect, I mean, this wasn't because of that order that the high school was integrated. This was on account of the expense was getting so big. I mean kids were leaving and going off to school. So if that was 1954, well, we started in '55, the council started in '55. We had so much work to do. So much—everything was segregated here in Fayetteville, so we started on. We were trying to get together to see what level we were going. We started with the theaters and the public meeting places. F. W. Woolworth used to be downtown, and we started there to eat at the counter. Now I wasn't active on that [particular] committee. We formed committees to work, and I was active on the theater committee and the school committee. The school committee was really my thing. And this all was started in sixty-, I would think '65, because the high school was already integrated, and we were trying to get the elementary level integrated. That was my part in the thing, but the council was our support. They were our backup, whatever. And the council—I think we had a membership, I mean of active people, about twenty people.

I: How many blacks were actively involved?

LD: About four black people in the community that was really working, and we wanted a change. We were working for change.

I: These were who?

LD: Carlos Carr and Minerva Hoover—she was a Carroll then—Minerva Carroll and Rosetta Dowell and me. It was just the four of us. Of course, . . . somebody has to start. And as things progressed, we got other members, other people in the community to join with us. And, let me see, my committee was the school, and I had worked on that. The League of Women Voters and the Jaycees were supportive of our efforts to integrate. Then we had several organizations in town that were backing us. And as I told you earlier, you know, [school superintendent] Wayne White did not want this. But the wheels were already in progress of rolling, so we got a lot of support. And we finally got the kids integrated in '65, I think that's when they started integrating at the elementary level. The Jaycees and League of Women Voters, they always had something in the newspaper every week about the integration.

I: When you started working with the school, who were you in contact with first? Were you in contact with Virgil Blossom?

LD: No, no, the school board is who I really worked with. I was the spokesman for the committee, and Phil Bashor was my backup. I guess we worked as a team.

I: Who was the superintendent at that time? Was it Mr. Blossom or Mr. White?

LD: Wayne White. Virgil Blossom was gone. He didn't want it.

I: So you didn't have any dealings with him?

LD: Not at all. I dealt with Wayne White and the school board.

I: Can you relate some of the early meetings you had with them and what you tried to do and how that went, how they responded?

LD: Let's see, in one of our first meetings of the school board, they were shocked for one thing, because the community relations council was meeting. We would work on our strategy, how we were going to talk to them. Nobody was to get upset. We were supposed to be very cool, you know. So we had to work on that maybe about a month before we could get it together. And we finally made an appointment with the school board, and we met at the Mountain Inn Hotel downtown. And it was three, let's see, I'm going to say it was three of the school board members really listening to us. It was at that time—I think it was eight people on that school board. But the rest of them just, you know, they didn't want to talk about it; they really didn't. And we appreciated them listening to us. Of course, I went on to tell them how far our kids were behind when they went into junior high. And we set up another meeting with them. I think we had possibly three meetings with the school board. And one time, the last time we met, I told them that we weren't coming back any more, I mean, because we weren't getting anywhere, and this thing had been dragging on for years. This was the time I told them I was going to contact Robert Kennedy to see if he could help. So, I'm out there doing my job, and Wayne White called and told me the board had been having meetings. So they decided, well, we'll do it [integrate the elementary schools]. I mean, just like that, you know. They said, "We'll do it." They didn't call a meeting for our committee or anything. They just decided they'd do it. It came out in the paper that the black children were to be integrated into the elementary schools . . . no black people lived in Root area or in Leverett. So all our kids went to Washington and Jefferson. So that's the way that went. There were no problems. I mean it just went on like anything else.

I: You had been working at integrating the elementary schools for seven or eight years.

LD: Oh, yes. All my life I'd been pushing. Just got a chance to really be heard after we formed that [community relations] organization. Because we always had something going in the community, but nobody was listening to me. And another thing that we did towards integration—we used to have to pay a poll tax to vote. I mean, we'd go—you know, everybody else, you'd just register. When we voted, we paid a dollar each time.

I: If you're black.

LD: Yes, we corrected that. We'd gotten rid of the police—we had to pay ten dollars for the police to answer—to respond to your call. Now people don't believe this—I know this sounds unreal to you, but if we were having an incident in the community, a fight or anything, you call the police, and when they come down, you had to give them ten dollars. And now I couldn't tell you who was on the police force because I didn't—I don't know, because I didn't like them. The only time I ever saw a policeman in my community, they came to arrest somebody. No contact with them.

I: In particular, do you remember any people who were particularly favorable on the school board to your ideas?

LD: George Tharel, he was manager of J. C. Penney's at that time. Henry Shreve was president of the school board. He was very negative. I think they just outvoted him, you know. I don't think he ever was for it 100 percent. You know, if you're overruled, you have to go along. And let's see who else was in favor of it. Hal Douglas. Hal Douglas and George Tharel. There was another one on there, I'm trying to think who he was. I can't think of all these people. A lot of them are dead now.

I: Any other people that were particularly opposed, do you remember?

LD: I can't even think of his name, but he and Henry Shreve were outspoken. They couldn't see why we wanted to do this.

I: What kind of reasons were they giving you for not wanting to go along?

LD: Henry Shreve was very outspoken about it. I think it was more materialistic where he was coming from. I don't think he thought that our kids couldn't learn. You know, just the idea of black kids mixing with the white. That was his biggest thing. I mean, after the kids were integrated that first year, we didn't have any problem. OK, well, after we had our meeting to have Wayne White get rid of Pearlie, Pearlie Mae [Williams], then we insisted on [keeping] the Thomasons. There were three black teachers [Williams, Romey Thomason, and Thelma Thomason]. And this was one of our requirements that those two teachers [the Thomasons] went along with our black kids. And everything just went smooth.

I: Did you have any face-to-face meetings with Mr. White on the matter?

LD: Well, he came to the school the night we wanted him to get rid of Pearlie Mae. I mean, we had a whole bunch of black people there that night. Nobody in the community liked her. I mean, we had had one teacher who had been there, I guess, about ten or fifteen years, Miss Minnie Dawkins. Everybody loved her. But when Pearlie Mae came in, I mean, she just soured everything. Nobody respected her. We just didn't like her. I don't know what her problem was. But anyway, Wayne White came over to one of the PTA meetings, and this was the time he shouldn't have come because everybody was up there, and he got scared and left. That was a rough meeting. In fact, Pearlie left, too, before the meeting was over. One of the parents told her that she could not come to school Monday, you know. We usually had our PTA meetings on Friday. And she was scared to appear on Monday. You know, there was a lot of hostility going around then.

I: So she was not eager to promote the integration of schools.

LD: No, no, no, she was against it. She was against it along with Wayne White and Henry Shreve. See, they'd march around together, you know. It was rough. It was rough.

I: Did you get the impression from Mr. White that he personally was opposed to integration or that he was just sort of carrying out the wishes of the board?

LD: You know, I don't know. I don't know about him. I think what it was, he didn't want a scandal. Wayne White was at one of those meetings when I told them I was going to call Robert Kennedy. And I think he must have thought that I was going to carry out my threat because he called me at my job and told me they were going to integrate. So I think he was probably pressured into it. He didn't want to do it, but he did, rather than have a big stink. Fayetteville had been going on so smoothly. Didn't have to have the guard [National Guard] in and all that stuff you know.

I: After schools were integrated, did the Fayetteville Community Relations Council stay together as an organization?

LD: Yes, we did. We stayed together because we'd have a crisis; something would happen in school, somebody get on the phone. This was a network we had. We knew the people—when we had a problem anywhere in town, we knew who to contact. And they would go in and talk to the manager or whoever. And we stayed together, I guess, about four years. And after everything got calm, we just kind of went home and sat down. Didn't have a crisis.

I: You served as sort of a monitoring agency for the integration of schools after the schools were integrated.

LD: Oh, yes, yes.

I: And you say that continued pretty smoothly? No major incidents?

LD: No, no, we didn't have any, didn't have any—our kids were, well, you know, at that time they'd been playing, we had a program. We had a Boy Scout and a Girl Scout troop. And some of the small kids had already integrated with the white kids. Wasn't any problem.

I: Before the schools were integrated.

LD: Oh, yeah. Yes, yes. Here's another incident that happened. Of course, I wasn't a scout leader then. What was I doing then? My sister was a scout leader before I was. Then when she went in to— she was a teacher of the kindergarten. We had formed a kindergarten, sort of like a little day care center down in the basement of St. James Methodist Church. And when she left the scout leader position, she asked me, would I help her keep the troop together. Minerva Carroll Hoover and I helped to keep the troops together. All right. We were having some kind of celebration down there in Prairie Grove, and all the troops in Fayetteville were supposed to be in a flag ceremony. I don't know whether this guy was mayor, his name was Honeycutt. OK, he was some big wheel down there in Prairie Grove. He was either mayor, a big council member, or something. But he found out the black troop was coming down. Juanita Fairchild and Eleanor Johnson and I were going to take the kids to Prairie Grove for the flag ceremony. He wrote the nastiest letter in the newspaper. See, we were unaware of his feelings because I had just gone to help the mamas get the kids' uniforms and stuff together. You know, they were the cutest things. Everybody had their little uniform. And they were so proud. And he would not let us come down there. And he called Juanita Fairchild. She and I and Eleanor Johnson worked together. And he said the troops could come down, but the niggers couldn't. So she said, "Well, OK, it's my trip. If the black kids can't come, nobody's coming."

I: The troop which you led was integrated or was it all black?

LD: It was a black troop. But we had all our activities together.

We went to day camp, you know, had cookouts, and all that kind of stuff together.

I: Is there anything else, Mrs. Deffebaugh, you can think about the school integration or anything that led up to the integration of the schools that we haven't talked about?

LD: Well, I think we talked about the kind of teaching that was taught to our kids. That school [Lincoln] would probably have still been there if we had been getting some good teachers, you know. The building itself was about to fall down. I mean, they never did do anything about that, upkeep and that kind of thing. But we were just getting some inferior people coming in, teaching our kids. You know, if I had not taken it on myself, my kids wouldn't know how to read today. I mean those teachers come fresh out of college and they come up here and party, you know. They didn't care. Wayne White didn't care.

I: About how many children, altogether, were in Lincoln School, would you say?

LD: It was a bunch of them. I would say at least seventy.

I: How many teachers?

LD: Three.

I: So really, the three of them taught six grades.

LD: Right, right. Then plus, we had a cafeteria. You know, the school system would furnish food; we had a cook and that type of thing, cafeteria for the kids. But we weren't getting anything . . . made me sick. And when they went to junior high, a lot of them just quit. They was so far behind.

I: I believe it was Mrs. Thomason who said that although they never got anything before, they started getting all new stuff at Lincoln right before integration. She thought maybe this was an attempt just to—

LD: Yeah, just an incentive to keep us there. Yes, and they was going to do some remodeling and all. We didn't want that. It'd be too late for that.

I: Sure. When Mr. Vandergriff became superintendent, did you have any relations with him at all?

LD: No. No, he was—I think he was a fair guy because the black kids in high school were in football and basketball. Our kids were really good. They cared for their team and got the school name known. William "Bull" Hayes was one of the big guys on the football team—really put that school on the map because he was a good football player. After him, there was always somebody else to carry on. Then the basketball team got good. I don't think Vandergriff opposed anything. OK. Well, have you been to the library?

I: Haven't yet.

LD: Yes, now, you probably will not see my name in that thing at all. You know how they leave us out of the history books. What you get now is just, I mean, direct stuff that happened. You know, so they're going to have it sugar coated. But you can check the library. Because my years might be wrong, you know.

I: Right. That's all right because I can find that out from records. But that's—the experiences or how you remember it is what I want.

LD: Yes, this is the stuff that happened. It really did. It really did happen. I didn't tell you about the time I had to go away to school. I did myself. But I went to Atlanta, Texas. Did I tell you this?

I: I don't think so.

LD: This was in '39. I was fourteen years old. And hadn't been no farther than Springdale and had to go clear to Atlanta, Texas, to go to school, high school. We rode the bus, the back of the bus, of course. And we stopped in, I think it was Mena—Mena, Arkansas. Hot, oh man, I bet you it was four hundred degrees. This bus driver —this is what—I've always known about Jim Crow and all this stuff, but never had direct contact with it, you know. Until I got on that bus, my sister and I, and the Hoovers, the Hoover girls, Minerva and her sister, we got on this bus, and everybody got off the bus in Mena but us. The man wouldn't let us get off to get water or anything. We sat there in that hot bus about fifteen or twenty minutes. Couldn't get off to go to the bathroom. Now that was my first experience. And I'm—leaving home, you know, you felt secure at home. Now you're in a strange town, know nobody, and then this, this bastard made us stay on that hot bus. Oh, that just made, oh, it just makes me—I tell my kids this now. It was first encounter with this stuff, face to face, just made you sick. And you couldn't call your mama; you couldn't call Daddy; you on this hot bus with nothing. He wouldn't let us get out and get a coke or anything. And what surprised me, nobody, nobody on that bus offered to get us a drink or see if we wanted anything. I said, "Oh my God, and this is what we leaving home for?" The signs and stuff were still up. This stuff is ingrained. You know that. And when you get with your people, they on the same level as you, so we just have to learn to survive together. So you make it a fun thing or you go under. You know. You really do. So sad.

JESSIE B. BRYANT

Jessie B. Bryant, born in Fayetteville, is a lifelong resident of the town. A housewife in 1954, she was active in efforts "to integrate the city itself."

INTERVIEWER: I just wanted to see what you remember about the period around 1954 when the high school was integrated.

JESSIE B. BRYANT: Well, that year the students were just taken into the high school. There was just two of them, and they were just taken into the school and put right into the classes. It was William Lee Hayes and Harold Hayes. And William played football, and Harold played basketball. And the kids, well, they just took care of any incidents that happened at the school. Now, when the junior high integrated there weren't any problems. You see, all the kids had been educated by their parents and by the community and they knew that they were to be educated.

The black kids were given equal opportunity in everything at the schools except for the choir. They would not let blacks into the choralettes group.

I: What kinds of incidents were there?

JB: You know, just the kids saying things. But the kids, they solved their own problems. They did not get sent to the principal's office.

Also, the black kids had to work against the stigma that they were not supposed to be able to learn. And the teachers would have rather put the students into remedial classes than to spend any extra energy on them. And once they got stuck into those remedial classes, well, they just stayed there.

It was often put on the black girls' charts that they were pregnant. If they missed class for any reason, then it was assumed that they were pregnant.

I: Tell me a little about the human relations council that you worked on.

JB: Well, we worked to help integrate the city itself. And the high school kids helped with that. They helped integrate the movie theaters because they would just go, and they would get in. Except they did not go to the Ozark Theater at all. All except for Wiley Branton. He was light skinned, and the kids told him that he couldn't get in. And well, he went down there, and he bought a ticket and he went in.

I: Why do you think that the integration process was so much smoother here than other places?

JB: The caliber of the people was different here. There were no farms or factories around, so there were no sharecroppers. The blacks here worked in homes or at the University. The blacks that live here are different. The blacks that live here are doing what they want, and saying what they want. The changes that took place here have been very subtle and sometimes slow. You don't know when or how they happened. You just wake up one day and things are a little different. And now, the companies and industry are bringing more blacks into the area.

I: I heard that the blacks used to have to pay a poll tax to vote around here.

JB: Yes, and so did everybody at one point. But, there was a man named J. D. Eagle, and he used to buy the poll tax for the blacks, and he would stand down there and tell them who to vote for and pay the tax for them to vote. He would be down there handing out half dollars on voting day.

STEPHEN STEPHAN
AND MARGARET S. STEPHAN

Stephen Stephan, born in Richmond, Virginia, was a professor of sociology at the University of Arkansas, Fayetteville, in 1954. An active participant in, and an acute observer of, the desegregation process, he wrote extensively for national publications on the integration of Fayetteville schools. His wife, Margaret S. Stephan, was an elementary school teacher and later a principal in Fayetteville's school system.

INTERVIEWER: I'd like to start out by just letting you tell me what your recollections were of the period in 1954 when the *Brown* decision came down, and the school board here in Fayetteville decided to implement the orders of *Brown*, four days later. Who wants to start?

MARGARET S. STEPHAN: Well, I'll tell you. You know, that was so smooth here. That's why they asked Virgil Blossom to come to Little Rock. He was real smart. When that law was passed—when it became law, he said it was law, and he called the principals of the black school and the two schools adjacent to that district together and said, "What shall we do?" And they talked about it, and I don't know that they made any decision, but he did. He said, "We will go to the black school and ask the people what they want." So the principal of that school got all her parents together, and they talked about it, and they said, "Well, we would like to go to whatever district our house falls." And that's what they did. And it happened, she said, that Center Street cut kind of right through "Tin Cup" so that they were about evenly divided, half went to Jefferson School and half went to Washington School. They had no problems.

I: Jefferson and Washington Schools were the—

MS: Two elementary schools. And, you see, no one [black] had been in the high school before. Because when they got to the eighth grade in the black school, they sent, the school board sent them to either Fort Smith or Pine Bluff, someplace. If they had relatives or friends, they'd [the school board] pay their way and send them to the high school so they didn't go to high school [here].

I: Why do you think integration went so much more smoothly here than it did in other southern communities?

MS: Well, I think—my thought is because he [Superintendent Blossom] asked the people what they wanted. It wasn't crammed down their throats, and he talked to the principals at the two schools that would be involved—the white schools, and he talked to the principal of the black school. And this is the law; this is what we have to do. And they all agreed with him—ask the people what they want. It wasn't crammed down anybody's throat. And I think politics here was—I don't think anybody was really opposed, do you think, Steve?

STEPHEN STEPHAN: Pardon?

MS: There was no politics here to—

SS: No. It was, first, very few blacks lived here, and they had the school, a segregated school, for years. Lincoln School.

MS: And they all lived in that area, what we called the Tin Cup, right down behind the old courthouse.

I: Right.

MS: And their school was in that area, called Lincoln School.

I: All right, now when was the integration process completed all the way through?

MS: You know, I don't know. I don't know when they started going to junior high. I suppose right after that. I just don't know anything about that. . . . I don't think they had—I'm sure it was not as smooth as glass.

I: You were a principal.

MS: I was a principal at Leverett School, but it was long after all of this.

SS: We never had any blacks there.

MS: We didn't have any of that problem because Leverett School, you know where it is, right there adjacent to the parking lot by the University on Garland [Avenue], and we were far away from all of that.

I: One thing I'd like to ask both of you is, what—I'll ask your wife this—what factors made this process much smoother here than it was other places? Was it numbers, was it the University, was it—

SS: Numbers and the University, I'd say. There were few.

MS: Yes, there were not many here. That school was small. Lincoln School was small.

SS: And the University integrated first.

MS: But, you know, I think the black people here were a community. They were not, you know, all around. They were a, I would say, they were a close-knit community. They had their churches in there, they had their school there, and that's where they lived. . . .

I: How important, if at all, were community organizations, churches, and institutions like that. Churches, how important were they, do you think, in the—or were they important at all—in the integration?

SS: They were important only in the sense that members of—a black person could go to church here. Very seldom I'd see them in church.

MS: They could go to the white church.

SS: Oh, sure.

MS: And, you know, I don't think it was any big deal. I don't think it was any big deal. Of course, I don't know how many children there were at Lincoln School. . . . But, you know, when you split that group in two and send them to two different schools, you kind of uproot . . .

I: So you think numbers were a factor also.

MS: You know, I don't think there were that many.

I: You said Mr. Blossom went to—

MS: He went to Little Rock. Yes, he—I think the reason they called him to Little Rock was because he integrated up here, and it went so smoothly. But, you see, I think—it seems to me [Gov. Orval] Faubus had a lot to do with that. Politics was so up in the air about it, and we didn't have any of that. Maybe he didn't know what we were doing up here.

I: The community at large seems to have accepted this rather well?

SS: Oh, I think so.

MS: I think so. I think the fact that they worked through the schools. Now, Washington School had the reputation of being *the* best school. When people came to town, they would all tell you, "You must go to Washington School. It's the best school." And Jefferson School was down at the south end, and it was a poorer school. Poor people lived down there. So when these people [blacks] were split and half went each way, I don't think there was any fuss in Washington School if these people came here, came to their school. . . . I doubt if some of the people in the community even knew it. You know, I don't think it was any splash or any fuss about it.

I: Just never became really a big issue.

MS: No, it wasn't. But I think part of it was the way it was handled. I mean he [Superintendent Wayne White] talked to these people in the schools, where they were going to go, and they talked about it, and he talked to the people who were going to go, what did they want to do. And, of course, the principal at that school had been meeting with these other principals, I suppose, in school meetings, you know. So they kind of knew each other. It wasn't like they were strangers. Minnie Dawkins was here a long time.

I: Now you mentioned Mr. Blossom. Were there other major people involved who you would say were responsible for there being such a smooth transition?

MS: Well, I presume the other people involved would be the principals at those schools. That would be Stella Hall and Juanita Caudle. And Stella Hall was, I think, the principal down at Jefferson. And Juanita Caudle was principal at Washington School.

I: As far as you know, there was no organized or unorganized opposition.

SS: No.

MS: I don't think there was.

I: Was there a strategy—you talk like a strategy was developed, and this communication being open, you think, was a major factor involved in the—

MS: Well, that's what she [Mrs. Caudle]—that's what I got from her. She thought that's what made it so smooth. They got them together, and they did what the people wanted to do. They didn't just say, "Well, you're going to do this." They didn't have a plan and say, "You're going to do this, and we're going to do this."

I: I guess what I keep coming back to is this, that integration was such a big deal so many places.

MS: Yes, it was. Other people, I don't think went at it like this. I think some of the people who were probably in positions of authority decided how they were going to do it and said, "You do it." See, people don't like that.

I: Was there something about this community, the makeup of this community, that was different than, say, a community in east Arkansas?

MS: Oh, I'm sure.

SS: I'm sure of that.

MS: Oh, I'm sure. See, we don't—we didn't have that many blacks here.

I: So people just didn't seem to feel threatened by this.

MS: I don't think so.

I: Apparently the high school—there was some opposition in the first year or two of other towns as far as athletics and things like that.

MS: Now that, you know, I just don't know a thing about that. I haven't heard anything about—I imagine there was. But I don't know. I just don't know. I do remember that there was some trouble, you know, they bused these people. And I do remember that there were problems with busing those kids to junior high, riding a bus, but I don't know how it was settled. I don't know how bad it was. I do remember that that went on.

I: But as far as incidents in the school or anything like that—

MS: No, I wouldn't know of any.

SS: No.

I: I've never read about it in any of the papers, going through some of the articles. And have read your article, of course. But what strikes me is the sort of matter-of-factness about which it was done here. For instance, at about the same time, Sheridan integrated their schools. The board voted to integrate the schools. There was such an outcry that the board rescinded that order, but it didn't happen here.

MS: You know, whether they published that here, I would have no idea.

I: It was in the paper on the twenty-second of May.

MS: It was.

I: The board met, but it was just a routine article, and I haven't found any—

MS: Any objections.

I: No. It just doesn't seem to have been that big a deal.

MS: Well, it was the twenty-second. I presume what they did. This was probably in the summer when they were getting ready for the fall term—

I: Right.

MS: And they got planned what they were going to do. Now I do know—I remember hearing Mrs. Caudle tell a story when I used to teach under her, that they got a new principal at the black school. And when the principals were having a meeting, they asked him what text he wanted to use. And, he said, "Well I've never had a choice." He said, "Where I've been, we always took what the white schools dumped." But here, the black school had always—I gather, I think—had been treated like the white schools. They had books the other school had. So they were used to, used to being treated like people, like everybody else.

I: So the idea of "separate but equal" was closer to being true here than other places.

MS: Yes, than other places. . . .

I: How much of a factor do you think cost was in this decision, if any, the fact that there was considerable cost involved, apparently, in paying for these high school students in particular?

SS: Oh, yes, yes. There was a debate about it.

MS: But you know, then, now those people didn't start going to high school near that same year I think.

SS: Pardon?

MS: I wonder if they started going to high school here that same year.

I: Some sophomores went in the school year '54–'55.

MS: I don't know that.

I: Graduated with the class of 1957, six of them, I think.

MS: Yes.

SS: But this business of going to Fort Smith and so on, that may have sped up the integration decision.

MS: Well, he's wondering when the integration came, how they took them right into the high school. I don't know.

I: Well, I was wondering also. Obviously, it was rather expensive to send these students to Hot Springs, some of them went to Hot Springs and Fort Smith, so was that a factor also?

MS: I think they went where they had relatives. They had relatives, and they probably paid for their books and tuition or they have to pay out-of-district tuition, and I don't know what they paid. I don't know whether they paid most people room and board or not. I have no idea.

I: Now, when you were principal at the school it had become integrated.

MS: Oh, yes, I wasn't principal until 1969.

I: What had you done before that time?

MS: Taught first grade at Leverett School. I started teaching there in '56.

I: And Leverett School was still all-white in 1956.

SS AND MS: Yes.

I: And do you recall when that changed, when integration reached Leverett?

MS: Well, you know, I was trying to think. It seems to me we did have a black child. I think we had a black child, maybe in the fifth or sixth grade at Leverett.

SS: I kind of think you did.

MS: And, you know, it got to the point—there were apartments built over near the University, and then, I'm sure, there were university students who came and had, . . . I just can't remember. Never caused any trouble that I'm aware of.

SS: They may have been Indians from India.

MS: Well, we did, we had Indians, that's right, too. The Colombes were over there; we had the Colombes.

I: Was there a sense, do you think, that people in Fayetteville looked at these blacks in the same way they would have looked at foreign exchange students and that there weren't enough of them. . . .

SS: People were that sophisticated. The numbers wouldn't make it such a major problem.

MS: I just think that the fact that there weren't so many is what probably saved the day here.

I: How did the community of Fayetteville react—and you've talked about this—when the black student came to the law school? You've talked about how the students reacted and how the University reacted. Was there reaction in town to that, any kind of unfavorable reaction to that that you recall?

MS: I don't think the town, for the most part, knew it [the admission of Silas Hunt, an African American, to the University of Arkansas Law School in February 1948].

I: But you think all that [admission of a black student to the law school] helped break the ground for integration of public schools or not?

SS: Yes, in a way.

MS: Very remote way, I think. Because I really don't think many people in this community were aware of a black man going to the University. The University was smaller, you know, and the community was a lot smaller, too.

I: So what I'm getting from both of you is there just never was a very big stir—high school segregation never became an issue.

MS: I don't think it was ever an issue. I don't think it was—I don't think anybody was really upset about it. Even the parents in the two schools where the kids came to school.

I: Was the fact that the school board acted in such a matter-of-fact manner about it, do you think that—

MS: Well, that would help a lot, and Virgil Blossom was a very level-headed man.

SS: Blossom was a big man in going to Little Rock. . . .

MS: I'm sure when I think of the people who were on the school board about that time—they were wonderful people. Very solid people. Ray Adams would be one.

I: I've got those lists somewhere. William Morton was one.

MS: Yes, Bill Morton. And I wonder about the man who was at—Shreve. Was Shreve on there then?

SS: They had these [black] people in their homes for [domestic] help, you know.

MS: Yes, a lot of these—some of these people . . . well, now the Mortons, I know, Bill Morton. They had a black woman work for them for years. Let's see, Ray Adams, I'm sure, must have been—probably the president.

SS: He's not around.

MS: Oh, yes, Ray's around.

I: Did you know Mrs. [Louise] Bell at all?

SS: Oh, yes.

MS: Yes.

SS: She was the principal of the high school for quite some time.

MS: She lives in Prairie Grove.

I: She was at the high school when all this came about?

MS: I think so. Well, I'm sure. . . .

I: Well, I appreciate your taking the time to talk to me.

LYELL THOMPSON

Lyell Thompson, a native of Illinois who grew up in Oklahoma, moved to Fayetteville in 1958 to accept a faculty position in agriculture at the University of Arkansas. Although he arrived after the integration of Fayetteville High School, he was active in efforts to desegregate the lower grades, as well as theaters, the public swimming pool, and restaurants.

INTERVIEWER: Let me ask you a few specific questions here, and then I want you to relate anything you feel like we haven't covered.

LYELL THOMPSON: OK.

I: First of all, can you tell us where you were born and reared and when you came to the Fayetteville area.

LT: Sure. I was born in 1924 in Rock Island, Illinois. We never lived there. My mother had grown up in northern Illinois, and though she and my dad met and were married in Arizona, they moved back immediately after their marriage to that area, and I was born there. Within a few months, we moved west to the Council Bluffs, Iowa, and Omaha, Nebraska, area—they are separated just by the Missouri River—and I grew up there until I was eight years old. In 1932, in the depths of the Depression, my father lost his job, as did 30 or 40 percent of the labor force in this country. And we moved south to north-central Oklahoma where we essentially took over a farm that was being vacated by an Okie who was going to California.

So I grew up in Oklahoma. My accent, I suppose, is more Midwestern because my mother was Midwestern, but I grew up in north-central Oklahoma. Noble County, Perry, Oklahoma, just about twenty-five miles northwest of Stillwater where Oklahoma State University is, in a wheat-farming area. I grew up on a wheat-dairy farm, general-purpose wheat-dairy farm, where I lived until I left to go to college in the fall of '42.

I might say a little bit about race relations in that community [Perry] of five thousand. I went to an elementary school up through eighth grade [which] was a rural school. It was a one-room rural school, and in the years that I attended, I think we had a minimum of seven students, in all eight grades. A minimum of seven students one year and a maximum of twenty-two in another of those six years that I went there. There were no minorities going to school. There were no minorities living in that school district.

There was a so-called "black town"—as it was called in those days, "nigger town" in Perry, and I suppose they suffered all the discrimination of such communities, but it wasn't so severe, I think, as in other parts of the deeper South. I know my Dad frequently took his car to a black mechanic, a kind of a private entrepreneur there that he liked. He was a bright and capable person; and we knew some blacks, not many, but we knew some of them there.

So that's my background up until the time I went to college. After one year in college, I went into the army in World War II.

I: You came to Fayetteville when?

LT: Well, I, after I went to the army—there's a racial story there, too. And then I was in the infantry in Europe, came back, and got out of the service at the end of the war. Went back to Oklahoma—it was Oklahoma A&M College then, and later became Oklahoma State University—and graduated in '48. I went to graduate school at Ohio State University at Columbus, Ohio, and graduated there in '52. I stayed on the faculty there for one quarter teaching, then took a position with an oil-financed foundation in southern Oklahoma and was there from '53 to '58 when I came to Fayetteville, Arkansas, the first of July in 1958, as a member of this agronomy department at the University of Arkansas, where I still am.

I: Would you explain briefly what motivated you to take an interest in racial desegregation here in Fayetteville?

LT: Yes. I can give you my opinion. I suppose no one ever knows exactly what causes their specific development. In high school, I was a good student academically. I'd read widely; more so, I suppose, than most high school kids. And in the army, I was in the hospital for a while, and then after the war there wasn't much to do in Europe, and I read widely again. The army had lots of paperback books that were good books—all types of books, classics, biographies, and so forth, and I read, and I suppose that affected one's outlook some. My mother, I think, also had a lot to do with it.

My father had been raised in the Southwest, where there were few blacks. I guess the big minority were the Latins or Mexicans, but he never harbored any strong racial segregationist feelings. He never talked about it very much, and my mother didn't either. She was, I suppose, on race relations, by her standards and her time, a moderate or liberal. I think the things that may have affected me from the beginning were the lessons I learned on my mother's knee; they stick with you and they're terribly difficult to unlearn later in life if, indeed, you want to unlearn them. And I recall the little Sunday School lessons she would teach all of us kids, my siblings, that God loves everybody, and it doesn't make any difference whether they're black or white or what, he loves everybody. And, I suppose, without thinking about it, that must have had some effect on me.

I can recall once, when we were living in Iowa, we were parked in—it was in the middle of winter, a lot of snow, and it was cold— and we were in a Model T Ford the family had, and we were parked in front of a grocery store where, apparently, Dad had gone in to buy some item or two. And Mom and I, and I suppose my younger brother, the only other sibling then, were sitting in the front seat of the car, and it was about dusk, and a black lady walked by. I must not have been more than four, and I can recall yet, saying, looking up at Mom and saying, "Mama, is that a nigger lady?" thinking nothing of the term at that time. And, obviously, I must have learned the term at home or in the neighborhood, but, again, it wasn't a pejorative term; it wasn't necessarily a pejorative term the way it would have been used in the house. And the black lady heard me. She looked at my mother from just a few feet in front of the windshield of the car—I guess the windows were down—and said, "You poor white trash, you ought to teach your child better manners," or something like that, and my poor mother was embarrassed to death. . . . So I suppose I learned something there.

When I was in high school, I was president of the student council, and one of the things the council did was to sell used books, make used books available to kids in the high school when school started in the fall. And I recall a number of black kids came up to our high school from their segregated black school, which was only three or four blocks away. The town itself only had five thousand people. And I can recall that I went out of my way to help them run down those particular books that these boys and girls were wanting as required for their courses. So I suppose that's a bit of a reflection. Again, because my mother was Northern and my father was Southwestern, I didn't grow up where there was much racial animosity.

I: What about after you got to Fayetteville in '58. Was there anything that motivated you to get involved in desegregation efforts here?

LT: Well, I think there was, yes, I'm sure there was. I had come here in July of 1958, and that was in the midst of the Little Rock Central High School crisis. I think it had started the previous fall in the '57–'58 school year, but the controversy was still raging. And I guess I was terribly turned off or bothered, or politicized would probably be the word, by the fact that the governor called out the National Guard armed with rifles with bayonets to keep nine kids, if that's the number, nine kids from going into school. It bothered me.

And there was, in Fayetteville, a group known as the Fayetteville Human Relations Council, and I went to one of their meetings. I think it was that first fall, or not long after, I had come here.

I: Fall of '58?

LT: Fall of '58, and there was a grand lady, still living, Mrs. Kyle Engler [Mrs. Thelma Engler]. . . . Her husband was a department chair on the University faculty at that time. He was chair of the agricultural engineering department, and she was quite active in race relations. She was a Presbyterian and had been active in Church Women United. That group, among women's religious groups—I think it's interdenominational—has been considered more moderate or more liberal or more open than some others. . . . I attended one of that organization's meetings. She was the most active member and chair of the Fayetteville Council on Human Relations, and she got me involved. I had a high opinion of her. I thought she was kind of a living saint in Fayetteville.

I think because of her and that organization, composed of a small group of people generally from the campus—white men and their spouses from the campus, along with black women from the community east of the courthouse that used to be called "Tin Cup," the black community—that Fayetteville was able to develop a small group called the Human [Community] Relations Association. I became very active in that group and remained active in it until the Fayetteville organization kind of folded fifteen years later when the federal government became effective in interracial relations.

I: How would you describe race relations in Fayetteville at the time that you first arrived here?

LT: Well, they probably weren't anything at all as bad as they were in the towns of southeast Arkansas and eastern Arkansas and those states east. Fayetteville had integrated its high school before I came here without any difficulty, apparently. Previously, our black high-school-age students, either on their own or with Fayetteville school district help, had gone elsewhere to other cities (and sometimes lived with relatives) and attended either an integrated school if it was in the North or a segregated school if they went South. Some of them were bused—I think this is true, a few years before it was integrated, to Fort Smith, where they had a black high school. But our race relations were more benign in Fayetteville. As I said, they had integrated the high school, but there was still lots of local segregation. The University, as you know, was integrated without any problems as compared to some other universities in the South, I think, largely because of the gentleman [Robert Leflar] that was dean of the law school at that particular time.

I: What, in your opinion, enabled Fayetteville to avoid the kind of turmoil that occurred in Little Rock and some of the other cities?

LT: Well, I suppose, historically, going clear back to the Civil War, we were more or less a divided area. I think we had about as many Northern sympathizers as Southern sympathizers here during the Civil War; but it was also a university town, and it was an intellectual community. The University had a diverse faculty—people come to state universities from all over the country, so they had a mix of outlooks, and they had people who were broader in view, and that was certainly different from small delta towns with no university, and it was certainly different from Little Rock. Little Rock was a larger city. It had no university. It had a junior college there in the 1950s, but no large university at that time. . . . We never had a large number of blacks here, then or ever, and that plus the fact of the people and the geography and the University must have had a salubrious effect upon the community.

I: Even though some state universities, like Old Miss or Alabama, responded to integration differently from the University of Arkansas, any reflections on why that was, other than those you've mentioned already? Was it partly geography?

LT: I don't know that it was any different. We may not have had as many racist legislators or politicians as those states. Now, we know the record of [Gov. Orval] Faubus. Faubus probably was, in the context of that particular era, not a racist politician. . . . His father was largely a socialist, and I understand he had a picture of Eugene Debs on his wall until the day he died; he lived well up into his nineties. Faubus taught—after he got out of high school, he taught school, I think in a one-room schoolhouse somewhere in Madison County, his home county, in a community that was largely black. I don't think it exists any more, that black community in Madison County.

And I think, incidentally, when he ran first for governor, and I wasn't here then, but I understand that he was criticized and chastised a bit by some because they thought he might just be a little too liberal on the race issue, which, obviously, was coming upon the scene because of the 1954 Supreme Court decision. And when he ran for reelection in '56, he needed an issue to run on. And I think he may have climbed upon this bandwagon to get reelected, irrespective of what his earlier training and outlook was.

I: Mr. Thompson, what, in your view, was the role played by the Fayetteville school board in school desegregation?

LT: I guess they played a good role. I was never very aware of it. It wasn't a role, as far as I am aware, that got a whole lot of publicity. I think they quietly and effectively, as far as I know, went about the integrating of the high school. It was integrated when we came here. We came here in '58, and I'm not sure what year it opened up. . . . But it wasn't a topic that was talked about. It was widely known and widely accepted but not much discussed in any circles. And I guess it must have been due to the leadership of those people on the school board at that particular time.

I: Let me mention some groups here and ask you whether you were aware of their existence and what, if any, role did they play in the desegregation of the schools. The Arkansas Council on Human Relations.

LT: The Arkansas Council on Human Relations was formed—I don't know when it was formed—I guess in the mid-fifties, and I think one of those people that was effective in encouraging its formation, maybe in helping form it—I'm not sure—was Harry Ashmore, who was the editor of the *Arkansas Gazette*; I don't know when he came to the *Gazette* . . . [but] he played a great role. He played a great role, and the *Gazette* itself played a great role during those years in not succumbing to the banal taste of the community and in attempting to follow national dictates and national law and constitutional law. And I immediately became active in it [Arkansas Council on Human Relations] and was on its board of directors for a number of years—I've forgotten how long—and it gave lots of leadership. It got a lot of good publicity through the *Gazette* and other papers, too, because often the other papers would pick up articles that the *Gazette* wrote.... Another person that played a great role in the Arkansas Council on Human Relations, so I understand, was Winthrop Rockefeller, who had come to Arkansas after World War II; he didn't necessarily want it widely known, but I think he often furnished the monies to support the staff of that organization. The small membership fees wouldn't have paid for very much, so Rockefeller's support played a great role.

I: How about the Fayetteville Community Relations Council? You alluded to that earlier, I think.

LT: It was kind of a daughter organization. Whether in fact or not, in any legal sense, but in reality it was kind of a daughter organization of the Arkansas Council on Human Relations. Several cities around the state had those. Probably the cities that needed them most didn't have them. But in Fayetteville we did a number of things early on. We generally just met and ate—just the fact that blacks and whites could meet and eat together seemed to be some measure of progress. We'd often meet in local churches and especially in the church student centers, the denominational student centers around here. In the Methodist student center, in the Presbyterian student center here, both on Maple Street. I think, and I'm not exactly sure now, but probably in the Episcopal student center, and especially in the Catholic student center, the Newman Center. The Catholics, bless them, and I'm not Catholic; they never had any compunctions. If we wanted to meet there, their building was open to us, and we did often meet there, and the Catholic sisters would often join the group. They were all heart with respect to race relations.

Can I go back and give you a little more background on myself that may or may not be interesting to you? I said after one year in Oklahoma State University, I went into the army in 1943. And at that time the United States Army was segregated as it had always been segregated. I went to Europe in an infantry division, and there were a number of blacks, of course, in World War II, but they were often—I guess they were always in segregated units. In a good many instances, they had white officers or maybe even white sergeants, but the enlisted men or most of the enlisted men, all the lower grades, were black, and that didn't work too well. The black soldiers thought that was highly unfair; I had a white friend or two who were officers in one of those black units, and they didn't like that arrangement either. . . .

In Europe, where I was, the blacks were often in quartermaster units and in trucking units and so forth, and there were a number of black soldiers, United States soldiers, in Europe who went to the army authorities and asked to be placed in combat units. And so the army took all those who volunteered, or took many of them, took a good many of them who volunteered . . . and gave them, in Europe, the basic combat infantry training, the same type that everybody got in this country in basic training—eight-, ten-, twelve-week, three-month, or something like that—basic combat infantry train- ing. And then took them up to the First Army, which was fighting, on the German-Belgium border about that time; and, as I recall— this is from memory now . . . gave one platoon of these black sol- diers (a platoon was about thirty-six to forty soldiers) to every regiment—now a regiment would have three or four thousand people in it. Gave one platoon to every regiment in the First Army —every infantry regiment, maybe other regiments, too, and the army kept that platoon intact. In other words, instead of taking individuals and peeling them off and putting one soldier here and another there, they kept them intact, which is what they should have done; I think it's good military training; they had trained together, and they knew each other. They'd have done the same thing if it had been a white platoon, I suppose.

And it just so happened that in the infantry regiment that I was in, we, our rifle company, were given a black platoon. So instead of having three rifle platoons, we had four rifle platoons in our com- pany. And they joined us, I think, sometime after the Battle of the Bulge or in early December of '44. I think it was in December or maybe January of that particular year—the war was over the follow- ing May. And I got well acquainted with them. They were a mixture of men from the Pennsylvania–New York area and from Mississippi and Louisiana area. They were an interesting group. They were colorful in language, especially the Southerners. I learned more four-letter words from them, but they were colorful, and they were friendly. The Northerners, the black soldiers from the Northern states were well educated. In fact, it was rather obvious that a good many of them were better educated than we whites who had grown up and gone to our Southern schools that, in some instances, hadn't been so good. I got well acquainted with them.

And, of course, in all that time—it was months from whenever they joined us till the end of the war—we were constantly fighting or traveling and walking through Germany. We were not barracks soldiers; we were infantry soldiers. The company kitchen would bring us up chow two or three times a day, depending on the situation, and we'd go through the chow line and . . . generally a platoon would go to one area and eat—twenty or thirty feet away from the mess kitchen—and another platoon would go over to another area twenty or thirty feet away, but you could eat anywhere you wanted to, obviously nobody cared. And I got to going over and eating with these blacks frequently and was friendly with them, and, obviously, they were friendly with me, and I became well acquainted with them.

I think we didn't exactly treat them well from the army standpoint. We often had them up front out on the point, and they probably suffered more casualties because of that than the whites—I'm not sure of that—but they were fine people, and I found them an interesting group. I was only about twenty then. That must have been a bit of a formative stage—you were asking me some of my earlier experiences in black-white relations, and I guess that would be a part of my formative experience. OK, back to you.

I: Let me ask you about one more group. League of Women Voters.

LT: Well, I don't recall. I know the type of people who were in the League of Women Voters, and I'm sure they must have been open, and maybe they did some good things, but I'm just not party to what they did historically in the community. I know that some of them would have been in this Arkansas Council on Human Relations and the Fayetteville Council on Human Relations and other groups that were open, but, as a unit, I really don't know. It's not that they didn't have influence, but that I don't know.

I: Anything else of general note that I haven't touched on that was significant about this whole period, this whole process?

LT: Well, generally, during that period, we didn't have a whole lot of support—not a whole lot of opposition either—and not a whole lot of support from University administrators. However, the presi-

dent of this University, who left here in about '59, John Tyler
Caldwell, was most supportive of us. He had grown up in Mississippi,
Yazoo City, Mississippi, but he was a brilliant man and well read. He
knew what we were doing, and he wasn't bothered by it. The dean
of the Arts and Sciences College during that time was Dr. Guerdon
Nichols, and he was most supportive of the faculty's efforts in racial
integration. All such faculty members, from whatever college,
thought of Dean Nichols as "our dean." I think some lesser administrators, lower-level administrators, and some of the college's
administrators, at least, were not very supportive or didn't have nice
things to say about this "race-mixing" that some of the faculty were
engaged in.

I don't know when black kids started playing on the high school
athletic teams, football and basketball. I don't think it was early on
in the fifties, and it may have been well up into the sixties, I just
don't recall. I do know that at the time my own son was in high
school as a quarterback in the mid-sixties, black kids were on the
team.

One thing we did, of course, we opened up, this local organization opened up the city's swimming pool. We won on that issue.
There were three of us—the local organization appointed three of
us as a committee. Ms. Minerva Hoover, a black lady, was on the
committee. She and her daughter, her older daughter (she had two
daughters), and I were to meet with the mayor to see if we could
work out some means of integrating the city swimming pool at
Wilson Park. . . . The arrangement worked out was that black kids
would be permitted to go in swimming when the pool was opened
at nine o'clock in the morning, and they could go in the pool for a
while in the morning—it was only kids who go to the swimming
pool. I'm afraid the city thought there'd be all kinds of trouble.
Well, nobody paid any attention. Nobody noticed. And finally, as I
recall, and my memory is not really good here, but I think somewhere during the early part of that summer the city dropped all
barriers and anyone could go swimming any time they wished.

We also worked out a way to integrate the theaters. At that time, I
don't know whether there were any drive-in theaters or not. There
may have been the one out on West 62, but we had three theaters
downtown, and one here off the edge of campus. All of them, I
think, were owned by the same management. . . . We decided that if
we could get a thousand names on a petition and took that petition

to them, they might say, "Well, gee, there's a large number of people here not opposed to opening up the theaters." So we got those thousand names. Then we had to find somebody that both sides had confidence in that we could give those names to and who would evaluate them and say, "Yes, these are honest names." We agreed upon a man, Mr. Hal Douglas, no longer living; he was active in the enterprises of the Fulbright family. Mr. Douglas took the names and started evaluating them. He started looking down the list and, amusingly, I think he got down to the fourth or fifth or eighth name on the list, and there was his daughter's name, who had signed the petition. Well, that worked. The movie theaters started opening up, first for a black to attend the matinee and sit in the balcony; but they soon found it didn't make any difference, and they dropped all barriers. I've forgotten exactly when, but they opened up.

We were working on opening up restaurants and motels in the city. I know that my daughter and I went on several Sunday afternoons—we didn't have nearly so many motels then—and quietly asked the motels if they would open. And some said they already were open. We got various reactions. Generally, they were nice. Only one motel, and that motel is no longer in existence, was adamantly against the idea of integration.

With restaurants I recall one amusing incident, funny incident. Again, the Catholics played a role. There was a nice restaurant in Evelyn Hills Shopping Center . . . [but] they never served blacks. So we had talked to the owners, and they were afraid it would hurt their business. They were really not against it, not racist at all in that sense, but they were afraid if they admitted black customers, there'd be a scene and they would lose business. I found out that they were Catholics, rather active in parish. So I went across town, and I made a date with the parish priest and asked him if I could come and talk to him. He was a magnanimous gentleman. We set a date for four o'clock one afternoon, and when I arrived, he served tea and cookies just like England in mid-afternoon. Finally, after the informalities, I told him why I was there, that this nice restaurant operated by a couple of his parishioners really ought to open up. I told him that I was sure that he and the church believed in an open society and that I didn't think anything untoward would happen if the restaurant admitted blacks. It was an upscale restaurant, and most blacks in that time were not terribly well-off financially. That restaurant wasn't going to attract very many [blacks] because most blacks couldn't afford their prices. And if they didn't open up, there would probably be a scene, a demonstration in front with placards, and that would be more damaging to their business than opening up. Well, he listened to me, and he was very polite. The meeting came to an end, and I went home. A couple of weeks later, I heard that a black was seen eating there at the restaurant. Obviously, the good padre had something to do with it in a nice, quiet way. I thought it was a decent way to solve the problem.

In regard to the integration of the swimming pool, I mentioned Minerva Carroll [Hoover]. She was a grand lady. Had she grown up in a different culture at a different time, she would have been a professional who could have made a great contribution to society. Her daughter is now well up in the Methodist Church hierarchy, wherever that is, New York City or wherever, and travels all over the world and is a great spokesperson for that denomination. She is a lady of mid-forties, I suppose, now, highly regarded in denominational circles.

I: Well, that's interesting. That's an interesting time to live through, I'm sure.

LT: I'm happy now that that experience was a part of life. This department [agronomy] wasn't very happy with me. The vice-president for agriculture then, who is no longer living, had been in his younger years a liberal, if liberal is the term, moderate faculty member on campus. But he wanted me to leave and go north. He said, "You should go north where people think like you do on racial matters." Well, I didn't go. My children were in high school. But I went about five years without a salary raise. Years later, when the University started coming under inspection by whoever inspects universities, the administration would say, "Oh, our faculty are very active in interracial affairs. There's Thompson who has been most active."

APPENDIX 1: FAYETTEVILLE HIGH SCHOOL AMERICAN GOVERNMENT CLASS REACTION TO INTEGRATION*

[1954–55]

White Students

I am not in any classes with colored students so I have formed my opinions from activities outside the classroom. At our Home-coming party a colored girl got up and led her home-room in a yell she made up. Her yell won. You would have had to see the "ear to ear" grins to believe the reaction. The colored students want to learn, but they just don't have the background of study that every white child takes for granted. The place for integration is in the first grades where children form lasting opinions. In our town there have been several people threaten to take their child out of school if colored children were allowed to enroll. Some people just can't seem to think of others and other people's rights.

The problem of segregation in Fayetteville High School has not been the problem of schools further South. There being only six Negroes entering this school of five hundred students, the progress has been wonderful. The students have accepted the Negroes. They are treated as any other student and are gradually being accepted into the extra-curricular activities. The students have taken the Negroes in wonderfully, but if this was a more Negro populated town, the feeling might be different.

I think the students of our school have pretty well accepted the Negroes. There is still a neutral feeling however, that is the Negroes are just accepted. They aren't made to feel they are part of the

*From the files of Fayetteville High School, Fayetteville High School Library, Fayetteville, Arkansas.

school or part of any of our extra-curricular activities. The students show no disrespect to the Negroes, but rarely speak to them or show any kind of friendliness.

Fayetteville Schools have a very small problem concerning segregation compared to a majority of the Southern towns and cities. Since Fayetteville has only six Negro students in high school at the present as compared to five hundred enrolled, you can see the problem is comparatively small. My personal opinion is that these Negro students should be made more welcome by the white students of the school by making friends with them and not being afraid to speak to them. The Negroes should also be asked to come to different school programs by the white students themselves. The general opinion of the students is neither one way nor the other. The Negroes are accepted by most, but very few of them try to make friends with them while a few (very few) have complained a little about it with no reason to back them up.

I do not object to going to school with the Negro students. I think they are most kind and courteous. I think that with great effort on both sides our relationship can be even better than it is now. We accept the Negro, but I feel we could do more to make them feel more "at home."

When asked how the Negro and whites are getting along in our school, I think there can be only one true answer. Since there are only six colored students attending our school now and our enrollment is five hundred white students, most of the students never see the colored kids. We seem to accept them in all our activities. Every student seems to be friendly enough to them.

So far, I think we have been overly nice to them in some ways. One of our home-rooms has elected a Negro to represent their room in the Student Council. The colored students all stay together in one little group. Most whites do not speak to them very much, if at all, in the halls. We have accepted them quite well since there are less than ten of them to our five hundred whites. Many times I don't see one all day long. I know I would be against it some if half the school was Negro, but since there are so few I don't mind. This is because I have never been in any other school where there were

Negroes attending. From what I hear, they get along fine in the classrooms with the whites.

I find that the Negro situation down South is much more improved than the school in the North. What I mean by being improved is the Negro students are accepted and in certain way brought into the school life in the classroom and in the outside activities. The white students don't leave the Negro students out of their activities. They join in the different school parties and other school activities. I haven't seen or heard of any trouble among the students.

Problems have been few here. We have had no trouble. Most of the Negroes are born Southern Negroes and feel they are not on the same level as the whites. They take part in our school affairs; however, they stay to themselves in the halls. Our school has just accepted the students; however I feel if more colored students were in school, problems would arise. Most of the Negroes here address the students very respectfully.

Integration in Fayetteville High School has worked out all right in my opinion. The Negro students are accepted by most all the white students. There are very few White students who resent the Negroes. The Negro students go around with each other and do not try to mix with the others. The Negro students have to study hard to maintain an average grade.

I believe that this step made by our school is a Christian and democratic one, and I am proud to be a part of it. Most of the students feel the same way about it. There are a few who don't like the idea of integration, but they have caused no trouble. There were no White students sent to private schools because of the move. People had thought that we should be integrated previously because it was costing the school board a considerable amount of money to send the Negroes away to high school, and, therefore, when the Supreme Court declared segregation unconstitutional it seemed very natural to integrate. Our superintendent received many letters commending the school board's move and very few against it. Of course, there was very little opposition because there were so few Negroes to come to school. One of the Negro girls led her home-room's yell in a contest, and won. Everyone was very pleased with this, as they were when the boy was elected Student Council representative from his home-room. A few white students have made friends with the colored students, but, generally, the Negroes keep to themselves. Of course, many of us feel that to be overly friendly will make them feel as conspicuous as being hostile. Nearly everyone has agreed that we should just treat them naturally to make them feel that they are a part of us.

In my opinion desegregation in Fayetteville High School hasn't really presented any serious problem. There are only six Negro students enrolled. These students keep very much to themselves. I am sure they are much more conscious of the fact than the five hundred white students. Heretofore Negro high school students have not had adequate educational facilities without going sixty miles from home. I think it is only fair for us to share our big new school with these six students. They are all very polite. They seem to have taken an interest in school activities. One boy was recently elected to the student Council. Two of the girls have signed up for the Pep Squad. In my opinion they aren't hurting a thing. They have forced themselves on no one. They stay together in the halls and the lunchroom. There may be problems in the future with more Negro students enrolling, but as the situation stands now, everything is working out fine.

I feel that the reaction to the elimination of segregation in our high school has been accepted quite favorably. I feel that the white students have just simply accepted the fact that we were to have Negroes go to school with us and it does not bother them. The Negro students have taken an active part in school activities, but they still keep to themselves. I feel that a few of the students are just tolerating the Negro students, but a large part of the students are glad to have them.

Negro Students

First I would like to say that I am proud to be a student of the Fayetteville High School. The first day we were registered, shown to our home-rooms, and other class rooms. Although in looking at our class rooms they all looked the same for a while. We could sit where we wished and we were treated no different from any of the other children. By being a new student, I didn't have any trouble in finding my rooms because someone was always nice enough to show us where to go, and to me it is both an honor and pleasure to be a student at Fayetteville Senior High School.

The things you think about when learned you are going to a mixed school is you think of how you will get along with the other students, or if you will like to go—things on that order. The day school opened, I was shown to my home-room and a couple of fellows came over and introduced themselves. When I would get lost in looking for a classroom someone would always show me where to go. Since I have been attending this school, I can't find any difference from the school I went to in Hot Springs, Arkansas in my sophomore year.

APPENDIX 2: DESEGREGATION OF FAYETTEVILLE SCHOOLS*

[1964]

Believing that an educated citizenry is the very basis of democracy, the League of Women Voters in the fall of 1963 adopted as its program "The Study and Support of Adequate Education for All Children in The Fayetteville School District."

The League's concern is that *all* children receive adequate help in achieving up to the highest level of their ability. Certainly this is in line with a statement to "Parents, Students and Other School Patrons" from Wayne White, Superintendent of Schools. The statement says, "The primary concern of the public schools here is the education of children in grades one through twelve, . . . Our philosophy is to develop every child in these grades to the extent that he will achieve at the maximum level of his ability."

The League is concerned also about the under-achieving white student, but this study deals with the educational problems of the Negro students in Fayetteville; primarily because of the glaring shortcomings and inadequacy of their education which our study indicates.

From our study the League members reached consensus on the following points:

Point I. The children of Lincoln School should be integrated in the Fall of 1964.

Study Background: The history of the desegregation of schools in Fayetteville discloses:

"1. Fayetteville High School integrated from the 10th through the 12th grades in 1954.

---

*"Desegregation of Fayetteville Schools," June 1964, Washington County League of Women Voters Record

2. The Junior High School grades were integrated one per year beginning in 1955 with 9th grade, 8th grade in 1956, 7th grade in 1957.

3. Since 1957 no further steps in the integration of the public schools seem to have been taken."

The following studies underscore the need for immediate desegregation, because length of time in a segregated situation is a deterrent to learning ability for the Negro student.

1. Negro children in Lincoln School, Fayetteville, test far below the National average in their academic level. In the Spring of 1963 for the first time Hillcrest Junior High received test scores from Lincoln. The National average for children tested in the spring for 6th grade would be 6.7–6.9 (6th grade 9th month) and the five Negro children who would enter the 7th grade at Hillcrest in 1964 showed general reading levels of 3.1 (3rd grade 1st month), 3.3, 3.5, 4.6, and 5.0. Communities at the time of desegregation report that 6th grade Negroes are on the average 1 year 9 months to 2 years 6 months behind the National sixth-grade average.

2. "A White Sulphur Springs elementary principal found little difference academically between white and Negro first graders. However, in the upper grades the Negro children were retarded. He predicted that much of the upper grade difference would disappear as Negroes moved up through the formerly all-white elementary school grade by grade. Other principals and superintendents, especially in rural and small-town areas, gave similar information."
"Other reasons cited were: Colored children come from overcrowded schools with less individual attention; live in overcrowded homes with no quiet study place and with little encouragement for educational achievement; enjoy fewer job opportunities and social freedoms, reducing their desire for achievement; and finally, were taught by Negroes who on the average are not so qualified as are white teachers."

LEGAL ASPECTS

1. "Separate education facilities are inherently unequal." Brown v. Board of Education of Topeka 347 U.S. 483 (1954)

2. "Primary responsibility for elucidating, assessing and solving these problems (of school integration) rests with local authorities." Brown v. Board of Education of Topeka 349 U.S. 294, 299 (1955)
3. Justice Hugo Black said in an opinion handed down in the Prince Edward County, Virginia School Case, May 25, 1964, "There has been entirely too much deliberation and not enough speed. . . ."

Point II. All the Negro children should be integrated at the same time.
Study Background: Mainly, consensus on this point was reached through common sense. There are so few Negro children in the Fayetteville School District that to integrate on a grade-per-year (or two grades-per-year) plan is unnecessary.

The enrollment at Lincoln School in the Fall of 1963 was:

1st & 2nd grades	22	one teacher
3rd & 4th grades	26	one teacher
5th & 6th grades	19	one teacher
Special Education	15	one teacher

If, for instance, the 5th and 6th grades were to be integrated in the Fall of 1964 plus the Special education class, it would leave a total of approximately 48 students at Lincoln School. Aside from academic, legal, moral, and psychological reasons for integration, it is unreasonable and uneconomical in this school system to conduct a special school facility for 48 students.

Point III. Because we feel all children should be allowed to attend schools in the districts in which they live, our members are opposed to the distribution of the Negro children among *all* the grammar schools.
Study Background: Dr. Carl F. Hansen, Superintendent of schools of the District of Columbia, says this: "I . . . believe strongly in the importance of the community school concept which is that a school serves a community and the children living in that community should be entitled to enter that school without any restrictions and that the flavor of the community-centered school should be maintained. *The process of artificially moving, or moving by arbitrary*

*order, children from a community to another community, I think, is
inconsistent with good education and good social and community
development."*
Along Dr. Hansen's line of reasoning, common sense points toward
keeping students in their own school district; for example:

1. No transportation problems.
2. Students go to school with neighborhood playmates.
3. No feeling of racial stigma such as accompanies pupil
   placement.

There are instances cited in *Action Patterns in School Desegregation*
that lead one to examine the possibilities of re-districting the school
boundaries. "Policies concerning free choice of schools, transfer
between districts, and districting of schools are closely related. . . .
Officials must consider traffic hazards and distance of children from
school. At the same time, they must try to establish lines that do not
result in accusations of gerrymandering." And, "Superintendents
repeatedly stressed that district lines should be straight, and whenever possible, they should be well established *before* a plan for
desegregation is considered."

CLOSING THE GAP—
ACADEMIC & CULTURAL

In a letter from the Fayetteville School Board to the League of
Women Voters the Board President said, "The Fayetteville School
Board has consistently worked toward equal educational opportunities for all children for many years and has made considerable
progress toward this goal. We will continue in good faith to reach
this goal as soon as possible. *We earnestly solicit the continued support of the League in this endeavor, and especially in the area of developing community-wide acceptance of School Board actions directed
toward this objective."*
The School Committee of the League offers these suggestions for
the implementation of desegregation of the Fayetteville schools and
for the up-grading of academic standards of the Negro student in
particular.

1. Focus parental attention upon school problems of their children, emphasize interaction of home and school environment, and educate the parents concerning what they can do to help. This can be done jointly by school teachers, P.T.A. leaders and school administration. Our study shows that while the quality of instruction is vitally important, motivation of both the children and parents is crucial.

2. Summer remedial classes offered by the school for all elementary under-achieving students. With only this additional expense, a group program raised Primary reading achievement from 46.6% in 1958 to 74.2% in 1960.
   This summer (1964) some League members and other interested people are conducting a volunteer program for all Negro elementary age children.

3. All teachers should be given a course in teaching integrated classes.

4. At least one Negro teacher or counselor in each secondary school would be helpful for Negro students. The need for these counselors is cited in several situations. In Charlotte, N. Carolina, "Superintendent Elmer Goringer felt that a Negro counselor on the school staff would aid the Negro children, who need to consult with someone of their own race." "Employment of the Negro teacher as a counselor, audio-visual director, assistant librarian, special education teacher, and assistant coach are ways in which some school districts have used the services of competent teachers during the transition period."

5. Residents of Fayetteville who are qualified could work with individual students, under the supervision of the school administration, tutoring those who have weaknesses in academic courses. This has been done most effectively by the school board in San Angelo, Texas and in the Ken Gar community in Maryland.

6. Use the summer months for cultural enrichment programs for the students in low socio-economic groups. This enrichment program could be carried out through volunteers from the community, perhaps.

7. Throughout the year, community volunteers might work with the kindergarten-age Negro children, introducing them to formal education and taking them on field trips for cultural enrichment.

8. The use of the city library should be encouraged and perhaps the library should be open in the evenings for study.

9. Churches might offer facilities for evening or afternoon study halls. This is especially helpful to students who live in over-crowded homes.

10. "All school personnel and community leaders should be armed with factual information, not only for the individual value in making adequate judgments, but because it is important at the time of desegregation in overcoming fears which often have no real basis."

It is the belief of the membership of the Fayetteville League that an understanding of the factors cited above, and a real interest in providing the best possible education for all the children in the Fayetteville school district, leads logically to the implementation of the consensus reached above. We believe that if the community is aware of the situation, it will cooperate whole-heartedly in carrying out these recommendations. We believe that the transition can be a smooth one, and that all concerned will work together for quality education for all our children.

> Fayetteville League of Women Voters
> June, 1964
> Dr. Wilma C. Sacks, President
> Mrs. Thomas B. Jefferson, Chairman, School Committee

BIBLIOGRAPHY

BOOKS AND ARTICLES

Acts of Arkansas, Regular Session of 1959 and Extraordinary Session of 1958. Camden, Ark.: Hurley Co., 1959.

"Arkansas." *Southern School News* 1 (September 3, 1954): 2.

"Arkansas." *Southern School News* 1 (October 1, 1954): 3.

Ashmore, Harry S. *The Negro and the Schools.* Chapel Hill: University of North Carolina Press, 1954.

Bartley, Numan V. *The Rise of Massive Resistance: Race and Politics in the South During the 1950s.* Baton Rouge: Louisiana State University Press, 1969.

Bates, Daisy. *The Long Shadow of Little Rock: A Memoir.* Fayetteville: University of Arkansas Press, 1987.

Bureau of the Census. *Census of Population 1950,* vol. 2, *Characteristics of the Population,* pt. 4, *Arkansas.* Washington: Government Printing Office, 1952.

Campbell, William S. *One Hundred Years of Fayetteville, 1828–1928.* Fayetteville, Ark.: n.p., 1928.

Freyer, Tony. *The Little Rock Crisis: A Constitutional Interpretation.* Westport, Conn.: Greenwood Press, 1984.

Gatewood, Willard B., Jr. "Arkansas Negroes in the 1890s: Documents." *Arkansas Historical Quarterly* 33 (Winter 1974): 293–325.

Hale, Harrison. *University of Arkansas, 1871–1948.* Fayetteville: University of Arkansas Alumni Association, 1948.

"Henderson School—Then and Now." *Flashback* 28 (August 1977): 47–48.

Jacoway, Elizabeth. "Taken By Surprise: Little Rock Business Leaders and Desegregation." In Elizabeth Jacoway and David R. Colburn, eds. *Southern Businessmen and Desegregation.* Baton Rouge: Louisiana State University Press, 1982.

Kunkel, Peter, and Sara S. Kennard. *Spout Spring: A Black Community.* New York: Holt, Rhinehart, and Winston, 1971.

Leflar, Robert A. *The First Hundred Years: The Centennial History of the University of Arkansas.* Fayetteville: University of Arkansas Foundation, 1972.

McMillen, Neil R. "The White Citizens Council and Resistance to School Desegregation in Arkansas." *Arkansas Historical Quarterly* 30 (Summer 1971): 95–122.

McNeil, Elaine O. "Policy-Makers and the Public." *Southwestern Social Science Quarterly* 39 (September 1958): 95–99.

Morgan, Gordon D. *Black Hillbillies of the Ozarks.* Fayetteville: Department of Sociology, University of Arkansas, 1973.

Stephan, A. Stephen. "Integration and Sparse Negro Populations." *School and Society* 81 (April 1955): 133–35.

———. "Integration in Arkansas." *The Christian Century* 71 (November 24, 1954): 1426–27.

Stephan, A. Stephen, and Charles A. Hicks. "Integration and Segregation in Arkansas—One Year Afterward." *Journal of Negro Education* 24 (Summer 1955): 172–87.

Washington County Retired Teachers Association. *School Days, School Days: The History of Education in Washington County, 1830–1850.* N.p., n.d.

THESES AND DISSERTATIONS

Benedict, Lona. "The Process of Integration in a Southern Small City." M.A. thesis, University of Arkansas, Fayetteville, 1967.

Dew, Stephen. "The New Deal and Fayetteville, Arkansas, 1933–1941." M.A. thesis, University of Arkansas, Fayetteville, 1987.

McNeil, Elaine O. "White Members of a Biracial Voluntary Association in Arkansas." Ph.D. diss., University of Kansas, 1967.

Vervack, Jerry. "Road to Armageddon: Arkansas and *Brown v. Board of Education,* May 17, 1954, to September 2, 1957." M.A. thesis, University of Arkansas, Fayetteville, 1973.

ARCHIVAL MATERIALS

Arkansas Council on Human Relations Papers. Special Collections, Mullins Library, University of Arkansas, Fayetteville.

Faubus, Orval E. Papers. Special Collections, Mullins Library, University of Arkansas, Fayetteville.

Fayetteville High School Library, Fayetteville, Arkansas.

League of Women Voters Papers. Special Collections, Mullins Library, University of Arkansas, Fayetteville.

Minutes of the Meeting of the Fayetteville School Board.
Read, Lessie S. "Lincoln School (Colored)." Manuscript Washington
 County Historical Society, Fayetteville, Arkansas.

NEWSPAPERS

Arkansas Gazette (Little Rock), May 22, 1954–August 30, 1958.
Arkansas State Press (Little Rock), June 18, 1954.
Los Angeles Times, September 12–15, 1954.
New York Times, September 1, 1954–August 31, 1954.
Northwest Arkansas Times (Fayetteville), January 1, 1950–July 16, 1978.
Orlando Sentinel, September 12, 1954.
Southwest American (Fort Smith), September 11–12, 1954.

INDEX